Captain Truman W. (Slim) Cummings flew bombers in the US Air Corps during World War II, and then for Pan Am for over thirty years. He has written two other books, *The Air Traveller's Handbook* and *Phobia*, as well as many articles describing his methods. He has also appeared on all the major US television networks.

'Captain Cummings has provided more help to more phobic people than any other single person in the phobia field'
Robert L. DuPont, M.D., Founding President,
The Phobia Society of America

D1420024

By the same author

The Air Traveller's Handbook
Phobia

CAPTAIN T. W. CUMMINGS
and ROBERT WHITE

Freedom from Fear of Flying

GRAFTON BOOKS

A Division of the Collins Publishing Group

LONDON GLASGOW
TORONTO SYDNEY AUCKLAND

Grafton Books
A Division of the Collins Publishing Group
8 Grafton Street, London W1X 3LA

A Grafton UK Paperback Original 1988

First published in the United States of America by
Pocket Books 1987

ISBN 0-586-07480-5

Printed and bound in Great Britain by
Collins, Glasgow

Set in Times

Grateful acknowledgement is made for permission to use
material from the following sources:

Time Inc.: excerpt from the January 13, 1986, *Time* cover story,
copyright © 1986 by Time Inc. All rights reserved. Reprinted by
permission.

U.S. News & World Report: quotation from the April 28, 1986,
U.S. News & World Report. Reprinted by permission.

To the millions of men and women who, through understanding and guidance, can release themselves from the bonds of fear and participate in the miracle of flight.

ACKNOWLEDGMENTS

First, my heartfelt gratitude to my wife, Carmen, who patiently and lovingly encouraged me in my cause. Her research has provided us with information about the characteristics of the fearful flyer and helped us evaluate the procedures that we use in the seminars. But more importantly, it is her perception, her sincerity, and her caring that has enabled hundreds of participants in our program to break through the impasse created by fears.

I want also to thank my co-author, Rob White. It was his professional ability as a writer that nurtured the idea for this book. He diligently organized and assembled a welter of information. He had a personal interest in the project because he had himself been grounded by fear until he attended one of our seminars. More than a co-author, he is a friend and an associate. Rob and I must mention our mutual friend and literary agent, John Wright, who found our book a home, and Rob's wife, Kaatje, for her patience and good cheer.

My gratitude certainly includes the people at Pan Am, who

ACKNOWLEDGMENTS

have been very cooperative in assisting me, my associates, and the passengers I have brought aboard their airplanes. I want in particular to thank Ed Acker (Pan Am's chairman of the board and CEO), Jim Montgomery, Jeff Kriendler, Jim Arey, Merle Richman, Mike Clarke, and Jay Beau-Seigneur. The flight crews, cockpit and cabin attendants have always extended a welcome hand. Captain Ned Brown and Frank Berry, directors of Pan Am's International Flight Academy in Miami, and their staff, have been very supportive of my work.

I have many teachers I wish to thank. All are therapists and all project a common quality; they care about those who seek their services: Robert L. DuPont, M.D., Rockville, MD; David B. Cheek, M.D., San Francisco, CA; Manny Zane, M.D., White Plains, NY; Diane Ronell, Ph.D., Boston, MA; Dorothea Leonard, Ph.D., Miami, FL; George Robinson, Coconut Grove, FL; Carmen Cummings, M.A., Coral Gables, FL.

I am pleased and proud to have had some special boosters. Ray Jennings has been number one on that list for many years. More recently, Marshall Stone and Walter Wriston have given my cause a substantial boost.

Thanks to my secretary, Gloria Chuck, who has given distinguished and cheerful service for the past six years; and to our conscientious and unflappable typists, Marco Pettim and Julie Varriale.

And finally, there is a gratitude of which I am conscious every day. It is to the frustrated people who contact me for help. Their confusions challenge me, and their glimmers of hope inspire me. I know I can help them. They have given my life a distinct and satisfying purpose.

CONTENTS

FOREWORD

I expect this will come as a surprise to the reader, but the first time I ever flew in an airplane I was as sick as a dog. It was 1942 and I was working in Victorville, California, as an air-corps crew chief on AT-11 bombardier trainers. One day, after we'd overhauled one of the aircraft, the engineering officer invited me up for a ride. I excitedly accepted, of course, but after we'd been airborne a few minutes, I almost wished I hadn't.

Those early airplanes were bumpy, hot, and uncomfortable. We bounced around in that hot desert air for a while and shot a couple of landings on the dry lake bed. By then I'd lost my breakfast *and* my lunch.

But I knew I'd have to lick that motion sickness if I ever wanted to fly my own planes—so I did. Very simply. I flew again, and again and again, and soon I left my airsickness behind and freed myself for a long, exciting, and happy career in the sky.

I tell you this story because if you're afraid to fly, as millions of Americans are, you can beat it like I beat my airsickness. My friend Slim Cummings, a pilot himself and a man who's helped thousands like you, has developed a technique that allows you to handle your fear so you can get on those planes and practice till it's a lead-pipe cinch.

Even if you've tried to convince yourself otherwise, your fear is your own problem and not the airplane's. Flying as a test pilot is dangerous, no question about it. But flying in a plane built especially for passengers, that's been maintained and inspected by hundreds of people, and that's being flown by fully trained and superbly competent professionals is not dangerous at all. In fact, it's a hell of a lot safer than driving your car.

I served my last two years as safety director of the air force, and I know how careful we were to minimize danger for our own personnel. I also know that as careful as we were in the air force, the U.S. airlines are many times more careful with their passengers. It's the plain truth that you take a greater risk by taking a bath than by flying in an airplane. Admit it. Your fear is in your mind, and that's where you have to go to get rid of it.

There's no reason to be ashamed of being afraid. Fearful flyers are often brave about everything but, and anyway, everybody's afraid of some things at some times. Was *I* afraid when my X-1A tumbled out of control as we were trying to break Mach 2? You bet I was! Did I get the willies when I was shot down over occupied France during World War II? You're damn right! I'd have to be some kind of blockhead not to be scared in those situations. *But.* I did what I had to do in spite of my fear . . . because I really had no other choice.

If you're tired of being grounded by your fear, or tired of white-knuckled flying, then *you* have no choice but to do what you have to do to get over it. It's hard to find the courage to do that when you're afraid. It probably takes as much courage to overcome a long-held fear as it does to pilot an experimental aircraft. But this book will teach you how to put your courage to work. Slim Cummings has put more than a decade of experience with fearful flyers into writing it.

It hurts me to see so many people stuck with this problem, and now every one of the estimated *25 million* fearful flyers has the chance to get this monkey off his back. After a forty-five-year love affair with the deep blue, I'm still looking for more people to share that awesome view from seven miles high. If you've never been there to see it or have flown too uncomfortably to enjoy it, you're missing the experience of a lifetime. So read this book, follow Slim's suggestions, and welcome aboard!

Best wishes,

Chuck Yeager

INTRODUCTION

An extensive survey conducted by a team of researchers from the National Institute of Mental Health shows that 13 million Americans suffer from some form of anxiety disorder, including phobias. Phobias are the nation's most prevalent mental disorder, being even more common than alcoholism or depression. Less than one in four phobia/panic sufferers was receiving any form of treatment at the time of the study.

The results of this report do not mean that all of you who are fearful about flying have a mental health problem or a phobia. Many people avoid flying because they have what might be termed a "novelty fear." For instance, there are repeated stories of grandparents who have resisted flying because the mere thought of it made them uneasy. They were uncertain (fearful) about how they might react to the unknown experience. However, an important family event like a wedding may finally induce them to fly. And except for some preflight anxiety before takeoff, they enjoy the experience.

Helping both the phobic and the "merely" fearful overcome their reluctance to fly is a major goal for all who seek to improve the quality of life in America today. It is simply not possible to participate fully in the wonderful opportunities available to us in work, recreation, and family life without being able to fly without fear or panic.

Although the biological mechanisms underlying fears and phobias are similar, if not identical, the important distinction is that fear is an appropriate response to current danger, and one that is viewed by the sufferer and those around him as reasonable. A phobia, by contrast, is viewed by the sufferer and those around him as abnormal and inappropriate to the current danger. Phobias generally lead to the avoidance of situations that most nonphobics do not avoid. In the case of the fearful flyer, this avoidance of the discomfort, or intense anxiety, marks the onset of a habit which, without professional assistance, is difficult to break.

Airplanes and elevators are regarded as specific, or simple, phobias. A much more complex and crippling phobia is agoraphobia. Clinically, agoraphobia accounts for 70 percent of the patients who seek treatment. Agoraphobia is characterized by spontaneous panic attacks, usually starting in young adulthood. People afflicted by it usually cling to familiar places and people, avoiding shopping areas and public transportation. After successful professional attention and treatment, some of these people may still have a fear of flying. Captain Cummings tells me that by the time they have completed clinical therapy and seek his help, they have gained a momentum and confidence that enables them to overcome their last obstacle to freedom: flying.

Panic, the acute and overwhelming feeling of imminent catastrophe, is not characteristic of a specific phobia such as flying. The phobic flyer may anticipate panic, but experience reveals that it does not occur. The anticipation of it, however, precipitates a series of "what-if" thoughts. The phobic anxiety syndrome is a malignant disease of "what-ifs."

With 25 million people hesitant about boarding an airplane, the fear of flying must be the most common of all fears. No one in the country has done more to help people overcome this problem than Slim Cummings. This book, *Freedom from Fear of Flying,* is a major accomplishment. It offers understanding, help, and hope to many who want to be able to travel comfortably by air.

In the past, the airline industry, the aircraft manufacturers, and the industry associations such as the International Airline Passengers Association and the Air Transport Association, have scarcely considered helping the fearful flyer. It is a common problem to people who fly, as well as to those who don't fly. The industry is being very shortsighted if it continues to overlook the needs of these people and fails to provide them with, at least, educational information about how to cope with flight anxiety.

Captain Slim Cummings is a hero to me. He has done more than any other person in the world to help fearful flyers "take off" for fuller, happier, and more self-confident lives. His new book is a major advance in his long effort to bring hope and help to the millions of sufferers who still avoid flying. I am proud to add my voice of praise and encouragement to his historic efforts.

Robert L. DuPont, M.D.
Founding President, Phobia Society of America;
Clinical Professor of Psychiatry, Georgetown
    University Medical School;
President, Center for Behavioral Medicine,
    Rockville, MD

A WORD FROM THE CAPTAIN

If you are afraid to fly, you have lots of company. A 1979 survey conducted for the Boeing Airplane Company concluded that *25 million adults* in the U.S. are fearful flyers to some degree. A 1985 CBS News poll found that 20 percent of the respondents were afraid to fly and that an additional 24 percent were "slightly bothered" by flying.

If statistics seem meaningless, consider some of the people who share your plight: John Madden, Glenda Jackson, Bob Newhart, Gene Shalit, Sam Shepard, Muhammad Ali, Maureen Stapleton, and Aretha Franklin—all of them are afraid to fly. Even President Ronald Reagan admits to feeling uncomfortable on planes and never sleeps on one, no matter how long the flight. The people I have helped include great-grandmothers, a state supreme court justice, a parachutist, the chairman of the board of a multinational corporation, and an Academy Award winner.

And yet, air transportation is far and away the safest way to travel. During the five years 1981 through 1985, the U.S. scheduled airlines flew *1.6 billion passengers through 26 million takeoffs and landings* with an average fatality rate of ninety per year. The years 1981 and 1984 saw only four fatalities each. Compare that 90 yearly to the 123 people killed *daily* on the nation's highways—an average of 45,000 deaths a year. Even after the highly publicized spate of air crashes in 1985, flying remains much safer than walking, which annually claims the lives of 7,000 pedestrians.

But the fact that there are 500 times as many fatal accidents on highways as there are in scheduled flights is of little or no help to the white-knuckled passenger overwhelmed by fear. As Einstein said, "Imagination is more powerful than knowledge." Although the fear of flying is not based on real danger, it is a dreadful feeling that is very real indeed to those who suffer from it. In the years that I have been helping fearful flyers, I have developed an enormous respect for their courage and determination to overcome these painful feelings and conquer one of today's most common phobias. I have also learned that even the most fearful flyer can triumph.

Freedom from Fear of Flying is the result of years of experience with people who are afraid to fly. As a Pan Am pilot with an education background and an abiding interest in psychology, I was always particularly interested in the passengers' comfort and satisfaction. As a passenger myself, I occasionally noticed a few people who were tearful or rendered distraught by flying or the anticipation of it. I began helping some of the people I saw in the waiting lounge or on the plane by using a simple approach that diverted their concentration on fear by means of a combination of deep breathing and muscle relaxation.

One early incident was particularly challenging and reassuring to me. One Sunday evening as I was standing by to board a flight from Miami to New York, a big man in a heavy coat suddenly emerged from the plane. He handed the agent his ticket, saying, "I'm too scared to go, and I know if I go back in there, I'll start screaming." The agent, seeking to unload his involvement in the predicament, motioned me over and said, "This is Captain Cummings of Pan Am. Maybe he can help you." "Yes," I thought, "maybe I *can* help." But I hadn't intended to put my methods to such a severe test.

I quickly learned that this man, whose name was Larry, faced the loss of his job if he had to take the two extra days required to travel to New York by bus. The agent told us that only two seats remained and that we could have them. I told Larry that I had a method that would make the flight bearable for him if he gave me his full cooperation. He hesitated, but as I gently took his arm he turned with me and we moved through the entrance door.

Once inside the cabin, he again threatened to start screaming. The cabin door was slammed behind us. My heart was pounding as fast as his. We crowded into our seats in mid-cabin. At first Larry sat on the edge of his seat, quite uncommitted to staying.

I immediately started to keep him busy. I told him to sit back and to put his full weight down. I made him release his white-knuckled grip on the evening paper,

21

practically prying his fingers loose. He was sweating profusely. I fastened my seat belt, and the flight attendant, aware of our delicate problem, delayed insisting that his also be fastened.

I ignored Larry's next threat to scream and told him that I wanted him to take three deep breaths. This, I assured him, would noticeably reduce his anxiety. As we taxied, and Larry breathed heavily, I urged him to sink deeper into the seat, to let go, and to relax. Although he still wanted to scream, he followed my directions and seemed less likely to explode.

As we approached the runway I asked him if he had a hobby. He told me that he played the guitar and had written some ballads. To my surprise, he volunteered to sing one. His high-pitched voice competed with the high-pitched sound of the engines as we rolled down the runway for takeoff. If our odd behavior had not already attracted attention, his singing did. We were a spectacle, huddled together holding hands while he sweated in his big coat and sang loudly, defying his fear with such courage that I forgot to be self-conscious.

Several minutes after takeoff, Larry asked if we were off the ground yet—a common time distortion that occurs in a state of complete involvement. He slowly wound down. His threats to scream gradually subsided. He took off his overcoat. As we approached our landing at La Guardia he even managed to look out the window. The whole episode was very moving for both of us.

From experiences like this, I developed a process through which people could cope with their fear of flying. I gradually gained enough confidence through these on-the-spot successes to plan a seminar to treat a group of people in a systematic way. I organized my first seminar in conjunction with Pan Am in October, 1974. The *Miami Herald* ran a story announcing the program, and the airline was swamped with hundreds of calls from fearful flyers. Fifty participants were accepted, and after a series of weekly meetings, the dreaded hour-long "graduation" flight, though stressful to a few, had its share of joy and triumph for everyone.

Local and national newspapers and television stations picked up the unique story of their conquest of the fear of flying, and for the past eleven years I have made a new career of helping thousands of people overcome their flight fear.

I retired from Pan Am in 1977 at age sixty, the mandatory retirement age for airline pilots. At that time, I was pleased and touched when a newsman wrote, "Maybe Slim Cummings has just begun to fly." People like you—those determined to deal with their fear—have taught me almost everything I know; it is my hope that you, too, will soon be "taking off."

This book is a completely self-contained course in overcoming the fear of flying. In it you will learn proven relaxation techniques to dispel fear in flight and will receive a thorough grounding in the facts of air travel and safety. Several chapters end with "discussion" sections, in which specific questions often asked by fearful flyers are answered.

If you've already tried "everything," do not despair. I regularly and successfully work with people who have tried and failed with many other approaches, including liquor, Valium, hypnosis, and psychotherapy.

No matter how intense or prolonged or bizarre your fear has been, the belief in and practice of the concepts in this book can make you a comfortable, even happy, air traveler. The knowledge and guidance you need to cope with your fear are here.

Freedom from fear of flying takes understanding of why and how the fear starts and what makes it grow. It takes desensitization to past experiences (mostly fantasized or exaggerated). It takes education to replace the ominous unknown, and it takes guidance to work through the impasse of helplessness.

The decision to do something about your fear is more than half the battle. The fact that you've begun this book means that the hardest part of your recovery is over. There may be 25 million fearful flyers in America, but only a very small percentage will do anything about it. *You* will overcome your fear; I am only your guide and cheerleader. Overcoming the fear of flying will have powerful, positive effects on almost every aspect of your life. So let's begin!

CHAPTER I

"I'M SCARED, REALLY SCARED!"

> People are not disturbed by things,
> but by the views which they take of them.
>
> —Epictetus, 1st Century A.D.

MANY PEOPLE WHO ARE AFRAID TO FLY SAY, "I KNOW THAT flying is safe, but I'm still scared." The usual—and most harmful—response to that is, "C'mon, there's nothing to be afraid of!"

In this book, you will be spared that platitude. Your fear is real. Your feelings are honest and your perceptions indisputable, regardless of how irrational they may seem to those who are not afraid. When that plane door closes, you feel you will panic. This is a real, physical event in your body; it is not imaginary. Panicky fear is the regular result of your getting on a plane or even thinking about getting on one. To say "there's nothing to be afraid of" is to deny these overwhelming feelings.

Your fear often starts days or weeks before a planned

flight. It may be persistent uneasiness. It may be a gut feeling that hurts, saddens, or threatens to embarrass you. Anxiety may produce nausea, diarrhea, or sleeplessness. At this point, you might cancel your reservation. Or you might manage to get to the airport before turning back. Or you might tearfully give up while waiting in the departure lounge.

If you managed to stay on board, the flight may have been a nightmare for you. Maybe you didn't move or speak. A woman from Philadelphia gripped her husband's arm so hard she drew blood. (Now she is happily flying around the country filling speaking engagements that she had previously turned down.)

I have seen the despair, the tears, and the frustration that plague you. You tell me that to fly at all you must get bombed or drugged or both, and even this does little to temper your terror. The trip can leave you stunned for days. As soon as you recover, you become preoccupied with the return flight. Trying to do business or visit friends comes off badly. It's a vicious, unceasing cycle, a ghost to haunt your very dreams. Many of you describe yourselves as "basket cases."

Even quitting flying doesn't help. Surveys taken in my seminars among those who had given up flying altogether indicated that some avoided going near airports, while others avoided even looking at a picture of an airplane and shuddered when one flew overhead. A schoolteacher I worked with was so phobic she was actually afraid that a plane might fall on her. (Since then, she's flown to Europe twice.)

It is crucial to distinguish this true phobia from "first-time jitters" or the brief stomach flip most people experience when reading about a crash or a highjacking. According to phobia specialist Dr. Robert L.

DuPont, "The common and relatively trival fear of flying and the disabling fear of flying are vitally distinct." He and others have pointed out that people who are concerned, who have perhaps never flown or have read a lot of adverse press about flying, will ask a lot of questions and be calmed by the answers they receive.

But if you're a true phobic, you are primarily concerned with the *feelings* flying—or thoughts of flying—evoke in you. You're less likely to ask questions, and you may have trouble showing any emotions at all when it comes to flying. You have a fear of being fearful, which is the shorthand definition of a phobia. It is very common and very treatable, as you will see. For now, let's examine the nature of phobias generally, in order to give you an idea of their roots and symptoms, and then we'll take a look at what ails fearful flyers in particular before telling you what you can do to become a *former* fearful flyer.

PHOBIAS

According to a 1984 survey by the National Institute of Mental Health, phobias are the most prevalent mental health disorder in the United States, affecting about 13 million North Americans. This survey also indicates that phobias and anxiety disorders are more common today than alcoholism or depression. So if you're worried that you're the only one with such a problem, forget it. As a phobic, you're no more rare a bird than someone who lives in New York or one of 11 million Americans who do business as sole proprietors.

You are not an oddball. But you *are* exceptional in that you have chosen to do something about your fear.

Phobias have been around throughout history and have occurred in all cultures. Certain fears apparently sent groups of ancient Greeks into mass hysteria. Today they are still common, affecting even the best among us. Some psychiatrists and psychologists suffer from them: Freud himself experienced agoraphobia. And although our rational Western world makes "irrational" and "fear" pejorative terms, there are signs that perceptions are changing. Today most phobias are socially acceptable—even claustrophobia has, if you will, come out of the closet.

"As a group, phobic people are intelligent, perfectionistic, eager to please, sensitive to feelings, and successful in school, work, and interpersonal relations," writes Dr. DuPont. "In my experience, phobic people are good husbands or wives, caring parents, and responsible employees. Yet they suffer from one of the most common but disabling handicaps. . . ."

There are phobias for almost anything you can imagine, including heights, flowers, fur, water, dogs, novelty, numbers, hair, and string—each with its own stately, Latinate medical term. Sitophobia is the fear of eating. Arachibutyrophobia is the fear of peanut butter sticking to the roof of one's mouth.

Regardless of the object of phobia, the symptoms are similar for all phobics: anxiety, even terror, when confronting that object. The experience—and this is very important to recognize—is the same for the phobic as if a real and deadly danger existed. The phobic person, quite naturally under the circumstances, chooses to avoid the disturbing threat. Therefore, "phobia" has been defined as a fear of being fearful.

Fears are common to all of us and to all creatures. They make us cautious when petting a growling dog or riding in a car with a driver who has had three or four martinis. Realistically, danger is present with either situation. Common fear is a useful emotion, a device for survival. It's sensible to be afraid of danger and injury.

So when does fear become a problem? When it's *not* sensible. When it loses touch with the situation at hand. Boarding an airliner is not dangerous, but someone who is phobic will feel threatened, tearful, over-whelmed, or panicky when made to do it. The psycho-logical and physiological effects are the same in both cases. Both are frightening.

I don't mean to say that your feelings of fear aren't real. Of course they are. But they spring from the fear of scary feelings rather than from the possibility of real danger. People who question your normalcy ("What's the matter with you?") or who proclaim that "there's nothing to be afraid of" have no understanding of the working of a phobia. Such remarks may only further isolate, confuse, or demean you. You are, indeed, responding to an irrational fear, but the response itself is real, honest, and genuine. As a phobic, your problem is that you get hooked on disastrous possibilities while ignoring factors that make the catastrophe highly un-likely. It's an inability to differentiate between fear and danger.

How do phobias start, and how do they become so powerful and disturbing? Imagine that after a pressur-ized, problem-filled day at the office, one that has made you feel down on yourself, you get on the elevator and realize—about halfway down—that it's very crowded and that you're pushed to the back away from the door. You suddenly feel closed in, trapped, panicky. At the next floor you rush out. This retreat gives immediate relief, and the next time you're about to get on that elevator, you'll think twice.

Although the origins of your fear are of little consequence, the continuation of that fear is dependent upon something of the utmost importance. All phobias are sustained and nurtured by a pattern of avoidance. The fear came out of the blue; it's embarrassing; there's no one you want to talk to about it and you have no idea what you'll do if it happens again—so why risk it? Future avoidances will likely follow.

But the people who have stopped riding on elevators or planes or both, because of their distress, find that their fear doesn't go away. In fact, it seems to get worse. Philosopher Bertrand Russell said, "A fear which we are unwilling to face grows worse by not being looked at."

As children, many of us were frightened by the dark or by dogs, for instance. Those kinds of fear usually dissipate as we grow older because of our unavoidable and continuous exposure to them. Similarly, mild anxiety about anything will often dissipate with repeated, even (sometimes) a single exposure to it. But a phobia begins to generate mild or severe anxiety once a fearful circumstance is avoided. With each succeeding avoidance, the problem is reaffirmed, the roots more firmly implanted.

FEARFUL FLYERS: PARTICULAR CHARACTERISTICS

Our surveys indicate that a significant number of fearful flyers are above average in education and job achievement. They are also perfectionists, which makes it difficult for them to acknowledge and deal with the humanity of fear. They keep telling themselves that fear of flying is stupid, therefore *they* must be stupid, which only intensifies their problem.

Flying fear may be so common because it encompasses other fears such as the fear of being closed in, the fear of heights, the fear of giving up control (or losing it), and the fear of the unknown. In my seminars, I often ask for a show of hands from those participants who are also afraid of elevators: about half of them go up. Half again will be raised if I ask how many are afraid of losing control emotionally on a plane or giving up control to the pilot.

Loss of control is a very common element in the fear of flying. Some people insist that they be in control. If they are in a car, they want to drive. They like to be in charge, and they avoid situations in which they must "take a back seat." Yielding complete control to the pilots up front in an airplane at 35,000 feet is almost impossible for them. In a Houston seminar in 1983, thirty out of thirty participants placed "giving up control" above all other air fears, including crashing and dying.

Another characteristic dread of many fearful flyers—and one that is infrequently mentioned but might well threaten them more than all other fears—is the fear of "making a scene." The fantasy ranges from "appearing nervous," to grabbing on to somebody, to fainting, screaming, trying to open the escape door, or "coming apart."

What else would you expect from a perfectionist? A participant in a Texas seminar told of trying to conceal his fear from other passengers. Shortly after takeoff, he was surprised to hear the man next to him ask him if he was afraid. "Yes," admitted the Texan, "but how did you know?" "Because," his neighbor replied, "you still have a tight grip on my arm!"

But if you don't fly because you're afraid of losing control, you *have* lost control. Were you in control the last time you "held on" for most of the flight? Or was *fear* in control?

Many people tell me that they "almost screamed," "almost fainted," "almost ran," "almost threw up," "almost died." The difference between "almost" doing any of these things and actually coming unglued might be compared to the difference between "almost getting pregnant" and pregnancy.

The truth is that in forty-five years of military, airline, and private flying, and over a decade of working with fearful flyers, I have never known a passenger to panic or become hysterical. Of the 2,000 people who have attended our seminars, not a single one ever manifested the bizarre behaviors that most of them anxiously dreaded. (More about this "anticipatory" anxiety in a later chapter.)

Claustrophobia, the fear of being closed in, is also very common. Psychologists have speculated that claustrophobia may be a traumatic consequence of prolonged confinement in the birth canal during a difficult delivery. Acrophobia, the fear of heights, also rates high on the roster of fears. This has long been considered a possibly innate or primary fear. Both acrophobia and claustrophobia relate to the often expressed fear of dying, crashing, falling, or smothering.

Crashes, storms, and turbulence all get high ratings on the fear scale. These particular "threats" will be discussed in a later chapter. The thought of takeoff was also revealed as a bothersome block. Separation from mother, or Mother Earth, concerns many—leaving the security of homes and families. (The agoraphobic resists even venturing outside the house.)

The news media's coverage of accidents and "near misses" was a highly significant focal point of anxiety. The inevitable deaths of 500 people in highway accidents over a Labor Day weekend is accepted and scarcely mentioned by the press, but when one lone student ineptly crashes a Piper Cub in a cornfield, it rates startling headlines. An aging and overloaded cargo plane that ran off the end of the Miami runway several years ago was front-page news for three days. One blown tire (the Boeing 747 has eighteen) will rate prominent space in prominent newspapers.

In an effort to justify their distress, fearful flyers collect and covet these stories. They seem to thrive on misinformation, distortion, and lies that confirm their position. Some participants in our seminars have been negatively programmed by the distorted tales of a fearful parent, spouse, or friend. Misery does indeed love company.

Those who try to cover up their anxiety or deny it

33

only make it worse. Few fearful flyers come to me with a story of an actual brush with death, although I have helped a handful of air crash survivors. Fear generates fear.

Most fearful flyers perceive their fear as *evidence* of real peril. Facts and statistics about safety are ignored because "after all, if I'm afraid, it must be because I'm exposed to danger." They project their inner fears onto an identifiable "danger"—the airplane—rather than acknowledge the enemy within.

This is not to say that all fearful flyers are entirely convinced that the things they fear are dangerous. Unlike the paranoid who "knows" he's being persecuted, the phobic usually questions the validity of his fear, and often this makes him more frustrated because the fear seems so "stupid" or "crazy." As Rowland S. Williams, retired major in the U.S. Air Force, put it, "A phobia is a fear that will not respond to reason—if it would respond to reason, there would be no problem because the people who suffer it are perfectly capable of reasoning."

CAUSES OF THE FEAR OF FLYING

Most people do not know what caused their fear. Some have said that the fear started when they left home for college, or a new job, or to get married. Others felt that the good fortune of a promotion or parenthood might somehow be jeopardized by flying. After they have had children, some people develop an extraordinary sense of responsibility, and being on an airplane becomes an act of outrageous irresponsibility. To a woman who has made repeated flights with her fatally ill husband to a clinic in a distant city, the airplane became associated with sadness and death.

A few fearful flyers have had rough flights. For everyone who has been on a "bad" flight, there are ten who say, "I've never really been on a bad flight, but I expect to be on one, and I always sit there tense, holding on, hardly breathing."

The reasons for your fear are many. They are varied and complex, and your reasons for not flying—or flying fearfully—are your rationalizations of those inner reasons. If a psychologist were to probe your reasons, he would find that *all* of your life's traumatic experiences relate in some way to your fear of flying. Although such analysis may be valuable for people who want and need to know themselves better, it has proven ineffective in relieving phobic symptoms. One study of 100 phobics revealed that although 80 percent of them had been in psychotherapy (an average of 200 sessions) none had been cleared of their phobic symptoms. (cf. DuPont, *The Modern Treatment of Phobias: A Review for Physicians, Other Health Professionals, and the Concerned Public;* published by the Phobia Society of America.) The vast majority of professional therapists agree that the root causes of phobia have little bearing on its cure. The truth of the matter is that the reasons for fear of flying are much less relevant than its symptoms—fear and avoidance.

If for some reason you *need* to know why you are afraid in order to recover from that fear, the reason may occur to you when you least expect it. A few people have discovered the root of their phobia in their dreams or in that half sleep upon awakening. One woman I worked with in Miami entered the plane but stopped in the galley alcove of the plane's cabin clutching her shoes. She explained her agonizing hesitancy by recalling that as a child, when confronted by something that frightened her, she would tuck her shoes under her arm and run away as fast as she could. She said that that impulse had just returned. She stayed on board, however, and after takeoff, moved to a window seat, where she became enthralled with the scene below.

In any case, the reasons for your fear might resolve themselves at a deeper level at some point in your recovery. You may realize it consciously, or you may not, but the necessary measures of integration in your psyche will occur as you overcome the symptoms of fear themselves.

THE SOLUTION

Fortunately, fear of flying—like most phobias—is among the most treatable of emotional problems. As Dr. Manuel Zane, director of the Phobia Clinic in White Plains, New York, puts it, "Phobias are common, crippling, and curable." The method for overcoming a phobia is the same if you've had the bug for twenty years as it is if you've had it for three months. This is so because the symptoms themselves are the determining factors of the disease. Learn to overcome your avoidance and confront and modify your fears, and you've licked it. In other words, *learn* to fly without fear.

Most people who are fearful of flying are also too frightened and confused to do anything about it. A woman who urgently inquired about attending a seminar was told that one would not be held in her city for another six months. "Thank God for that," she said. Others insist that it is not safe to fly, and remain grounded. Some just keep hoping the problem will go away.

Each phobic believes his particular fear and suffering is unique. You have a repeated, habitual, uncontrollable overresponse when even contemplating a flight. You are afraid of being afraid. And every time you run away from the threat, it exerts a tighter hold. Running away from a plane is easy, and it has one immediate compensation—escape! I've witnessed it many times. That first feeling is great relief. The second is discouragement. Your feelings of fear won out over your best intentions.

But if flying is important enough to you, your family, your job, and your self-esteem, you can change. What does your fear of flying cost you? Are you missing out on fun vacations, exotic travel opportunities? Do you waste valuable business hours driving to distant cities that are much nearer by plane? Have promotions passed you by because you have been unable to take on new responsibilities that require flying? Or do you fly, but in great agony? Is the experience of flying so miserable that it outweighs all benefits? Wouldn't you be happier if you could comfortably use the safest form of transportation today—the airplane?

The antidote to avoidance is gentle, supportive, and

knowledgeable confrontation. There is no alternative. You have been tricked by your feelings, and the time has come to call their bluff.

In the next chapter, I will show you how to confront your fear and dispel it. As one former fearful flyer said, "As long as I locked my fear up, it would beat on the door and threaten me. Finally, I opened that door and found, not a lion, but a pussycat."

DISCUSSION

Besides a psychologist, or a phobia clinic, where might I seek help?

Contact the major airlines that serve your city to determine if they have a program for fearful flyers. Mental health associations can give you some guidance. You may need clinical help if you are generally fearful, or reluctant to leave home.

I'm not really afraid of flying. I'm afraid of being closed in on that airplane, or anywhere I can't get out.

Your comment is one that I hear often. Fear of being closed in, fear of heights, and fear of giving up control are all fears that relate to flying. People who are phobic like the option of an open door, an avenue of escape. That alternative is not available on an aircraft. It *is* available in an elevator. Start confronting elevators— using the coping tools taught in Chapter II—by just looking at one, touching it, opening and closing the door, quickly stepping in and out. Get a companion to help you. Pick a time when the elevator is little used.

Maybe ten minutes of exposure a day is enough for the first week. Remember, three steps forward and one back is still two steps forward. It has been my experience in working with people with a problem similar to yours that the fear of confinement is a projection that fades away once it is completely confronted. I like to quote a Texas friend who said, "I held on to my fears of being closed in until I realized that that fear had closed me out of many travel opportunities."

Heights really bother me. I never go above the second floor of any building and the thought of being several miles up in the sky really frightens me. I recently had a nightmare about flying and I woke up in a cold sweat.

The most common nightmares are about falling. The fear of falling seems to be innate. In one study, several babies were placed on a large glass-top table and, upon looking down, were noted to exhibit "a significant startle response." Many pilots are afraid of standing on a cliff or near the edge of the roof of a tall building. They are not similarly affected in an airplane. The rare passenger who complains about this problem in flight is the one who has avoided looking out. Again, confrontation is the only solution.

My fear isn't too bad once we get off the ground. My problem is the torture I put myself through the week before the flight. I get diarrhea, I am irritable, and the night before the flight I hardly sleep.

Phobic flyers create most of their misery with this kind of projection. They anticipate a severe problem and dwell obsessively on it. Some fantasize crashing or dying, some see themselves as losing emotional control, and some see themselves, at the very least, embarrassed by tears and conspicuous behavior. Psychiatrist Fritz Perls called anxiety "the gap between the now and the future."

Heights and being closed in don't bother me. Not being in control is what bothers me most. I'm a good and careful driver, and I feel safe when I am driving.

Are you really in control? Let's suppose that your car is in perfect condition and that you are sober, alert, and the best driver in the state of Florida. People who are safe, competent, and cautious drivers like you are getting wiped out every day by someone coming up behind them or speeding toward them in an unsafe car driven recklessly, angrily, carelessly, or sleepily. Drunken driving accounts for half of the more than 45,000 people killed annually on our highways. I don't want to scare you out of driving, but your competence at the wheel can be severely jeopardized by other drivers' incompetence. It can make you nervous to give up control to the pilots up front on your next flight, but I can promise you that they are competently, soberly, and carefully driving an air machine that is as infallible as man has, as yet, been able to devise.

I've had my fear of flying for a long time, and all I ever do about it is wish it would go away. I wonder if there is a payoff to keeping it.

You're the only one who can answer that. I suggest that you get two pieces of paper. On one write down all the reasons, or "payoffs," for you to continue to avoid flying. Be honest. On the other, list the advantages of being able to travel by air.

A woman in Chicago admitted that she was made to feel very important every year at Christmas time when her husband and children would futilely beg her to fly to Florida with them. A man in Boston said that his frightening, but amusing, stories about flying always made him the center of attention at cocktail parties. He loved that attention and was reluctant to give it up.

But the fear of flying can also be a factor in strained marital relations or even divorce. The husband or wife who loves to travel may eventually find someone else to travel with if the spouse keeps refusing travel opportunities.

Many people have said that booze is what got them through the flight. Your comments?

A mild drink or sedative might help a mild anxiety. People who seek my help have found that it doesn't release them from the grip of their fear. One man told me that even after a dozen martinis he was still both sober and scared during the whole flight. After landing, the liquor took effect, and he suddenly was so drunk that two attendants had to help him disembark.

Have you ever worked with any people who have experienced an actual crash?

Yes. Interestingly enough, despite the reality of their trauma, they got along just as well as those who had never had a close call but had fantasized a traumatic experience.

Soon after my recent divorce, I developed a fear of flying. I called a psychologist friend and he told me to get back on another airplane and, instead of trying to be unafraid, try to be as afraid as I could. Isn't this a rough way for me to attack my fear?

Talk with your friend about it. Some therapists have

good results using this method, which is called "flooding" or "implosion." The idea is to encounter your phobia head-on, even try to intensify the fear reactions, until it goes away. The method deals directly and uncompromisingly with the problem. The desensitization techniques presented in this book are more gentle and more permissive.

CHAPTER II

THE ANTIDOTE
TO FEAR

> Neils Bohr, the Nobel physicist, had a horseshoe
> hanging over his desk. When asked if he believed
> the horseshoe would bring him good luck, Bohr
> replied, "Not at all. I am scarcely likely to
> believe in such foolish nonsense. However, I am
> told that a horseshoe will bring you good luck
> whether you believe in it or not."

YOUR FEAR OF FLYING HAS BECOME A HABIT THAT HAS
imprisoned or at least restricted you. It probably grew
insidiously until suddenly it presented itself as an
insurmountable threat. Then the avoidance pattern set
in: you got off a plane once and you haven't been on
one since.

Now some people say, "But I fly. I am not avoiding
an airplane." Yes, but when phobic people force themselves to fly, doing so under great pressure, they still try
to avoid the experience of flight. They try to avoid it
with liquor or Valium, or by holding on to their
armrests, or by closing their eyes.

This resistance leads to an exhausting, miserable experience. The devices of avoidance are counter-productive. They only reinforce the problem. It takes courage to try to fly in such a state, of course, but it's wasted courage. You cannot conquer phobia with guts alone. You must be aware of how your fear builds inside of you and what it does to you physically and psychologically. To confront your phobia, you need coping tools, and in using these tools, you must aim for *motivation, understanding, honesty,* and *practice* in order to overcome your fear.

Motivation: Taking the first step—believing that it's worth the trouble to help yourself—is the biggest hurdle you have to clear.

A man in Chicago announced: "I'm fed up with dodging my fear. I may make an ass of myself tomorrow, but I'm going to be on that airplane!" A woman told me, "There isn't any way I'm going to see my grandchildren in California unless I fly out there. I'm going to do it!" A schoolteacher drove a beat-up old Ford a thousand miles to attend a seminar in Los Angeles. A prospective bridegroom made his first flight with us because his bride-to-be told him, "We'll fly to Bermuda for our honeymoon, or nothing!" A psychiatrist joined one of our seminars because, he said, "I'm embarrassed. I treat other people for the problem, but I am unable to help myself." Many other people just say they are sick and tired of being afraid.

It doesn't make any difference how long or how severely you've been afraid. If you *want* to overcome it, it's not really that difficult. The most important thing is to make the first move.

Understanding: Understand how your fear starts, how it builds, how it affects you, and what you can do about it. Understand the big parts played by anticipation, anxiety, and avoidance. Understand that the problem is not external—it is not the airplane or the crew, or the mechanics or the controllers that cause your problem (see Chapter IV: Flying Today). The problem is internal, caused by the emotions you have created. Understand that change is possible and that changing will enrich your life. Understand that the tools for coping are all here for you. Understand that practice and determination can counter the habitual pattern established by many years of inaction.

Honesty: This is a tough one. It is easier to be honest with others than it is to be honest with yourself. Honesty means taking responsibility for your fear—not blaming it on an overprotective mother, an unsympathetic spouse, or a boss who is pressing you to expand your territory. Honesty means the courage to reexamine the excuses you have used to justify your fear. You might find that the underlying fear is really the fear of being fearful. There is honesty also in admitting that you are fearful and choosing not to do anything about it.

Practice: One woman recently told me, "All those preflight activities are a long way from the real thing. I can do those exercises, look at airplanes, even sit on one that's parked. My trouble is not on the ground, it's in the air." Agreed. There's a big difference between the dress rehearsal and opening night. Be that as it may, practicing the exercises in this chapter is as close as you can get to the real thing. Only through practice, through simulated experience, can you bridge the gap.

Fear may be compared to a weed. If left alone, a weed will grow and spread. Fear, if uncontrolled, will grow too—and frustrate you. Your response until now has been habitual: "If it flies, I'm not going on it!" or "I'll hold on until we land and then thank God we made it!" You have been unaware of a choice in the matter. The psychologist Rollo May once wrote, "Human freedom involves our capacity to pause between stimulus and response. And, in that pause, to choose the response towards which we wish to throw our weight." Practicing appropriate antidotes to fear will give you that choice.

TRIPLE A/BM

The antidote to fear can be summarized in the formula: Triple A/BM. This may sound gimmicky, but it's an easy way to remember the crux of what I have to tell you about dealing with fear. An easily remembered formula will stand you in good stead when your fear is trying to have a field day with you.

Triple A stands for *acknowledgment, acceptance,* and *action;* BM for the *kind* of action you take: namely, *breathing* and *movement.* Everything you have learned and will learn in this book will boil down to Triple

A/BM. Think of it as your safety net, your magic pill. Once it's learned and safely in your head, you will be able to fly comfortably, knowing that you have a proven, sure-fire way to deal with your fear.

Acknowledgment: The moment you begin to tighten up, whether it be on the plane, in the boarding lounge, on the phone confirming a flight reservation, or trying to get to sleep the night before a flight, *acknowledge* that *your feelings,* not the airplane, are at the root of your problem. In this book you will find ample evidence for the safety of air travel, but in the end you must realize that you cannot change the airplane. You can, however, alter your reactions to it. That responsibility is yours. I will show you how to accept it. For now, let the pilot fly the plane and learn how to handle yourself when you're on one. Acknowledgment itself won't necessarily ease your fear, but it will put the focus where it belongs.

If you are to overcome your fear of flying, you will have to change. Change can be uncomfortable at first. You must recognize that you have been programming yourself negatively about flying and that you will have to challenge that programming with new programming. Until now, you have been reinforcing your fear. You don't look for any *good* stories about flying or its safety, you look for *bad* stories in order to confirm your fear. You have been dwelling on "I can't fly"; "I'm really too afraid"; "My case is different." That's the kind of garbage you've put into that little computer between your ears. What comes out? Fear. Now we must start putting new information, facts, and hope in there instead.

FREEDOM FROM FEAR OF FLYING

So be aware: you are often afraid of what you *think* might happen on an airplane while the majority of your co-passengers and the flight crew are blithely going about their business. Turbulence, as you will see, is certainly not dangerous. Nor are sharp turns. Changing the power in the engines is not dangerous. Takeoff is not dangerous. Be aware of what *you have made* out of the experience of flight.

We are what we think. Our thoughts are the source of our character, our creativity, our joy, our depression, our fear. Thoughts create feelings and feelings create fear. That is an indisputable sequence. Most fearful flyers feed their thoughts with hypothetical, unrealistic thinking—with negative thoughts. You must become *aware* of how you feed your fear before you can starve it. So welcome fear into your kitchen, but don't offer it tea.

You will have learned all I have to tell you about acknowledging your fear if—when confronted by those tightening, trembling moments—you step back for an instant and say to yourself, "I know what this is. I've had these feelings before. They come from me, not from the airplane." Once you've made this first step you can move on to . . .

Acceptance: Fearful flyers tend not to accept their feelings. They want to shut them off, to be rid of them entirely and immediately. Trying to squash your fears simply increases the threatening feelings. Only when you accept fear can you begin to deal with it effectively. Feelings, as scary as they might be, won't disable you. No one ever got a heart attack from being nervous. Feelings won't embarrass you or demean you if you recognize them as transient human phenomena. Your fear bothers you precisely as much as you permit it. In a very real sense, fear is the only thing you tackle when you get on a plane.

An old prayer that is now one of the basic tenets of Alcoholics Anonymous applies equally to fearful flyers: "God grant me the serenity to accept the things I cannot change, the courage to change the things I can, and the wisdom to know the difference." If your attitude is, "I'll listen. I'll try to follow suggestions," you'll make it. Tell yourself, "I'm not a coward, only a frightened skeptic. And instead of trying to lick this thing all at once, I'm going to take it one day at a time." Once you've accepted your fear, you are free to take . . .

Action: In the past you have *re*acted. You have been inundated with sensations—with rapid heartbeats, shallow breathing, tightness in your throat and guts, sweating, and shaky knees. The reactions to danger, real or imagined, are always the same. They are alarming because they seem to be uncontrollable—they just happen to you.

Scientists believe that these responses, which are common to *all* people in certain circumstances, are left over from the primitive "fight or flight" response of our constantly endangered simian ancestors who often faced threats to their survival. But how do you take "flight" from your seat in a 747 en route from New York to London? How can you "fight" with that invisible demon that shows up inside you every time flying is mentioned? You cannot, in any conventional sense, and that's why you get so churned up inside. What you *can* do is address the physical symptoms of fear directly to moderate and eventually diminish them.

You are going to learn how to *act* to interrupt and dissipate your *r*eactions to flight.

Your first act is to find yourself a partner. From this point on, your preparation for flight will be a two-person job. It is possible to do it on your own, but the entire experience will be less lonely, and more pleasant, if you have a friend along.

Be careful in selecting your partner. Choose someone who is *not* afraid to fly but who is familiar with you and your problems. Spouses, friends, and relatives are all likely candidates, but the person who is most caring, patient, and understanding will be your best choice. A sense of humor will help enormously. In addition to a three-hour assignment at the outset, your partner should be prepared to spend a couple of hours with you about three times a week for several weeks and then join you on a flight to and from a destination of your choice for a day or a weekend. This is a big commitment of time and effort. Make sure that your partner knows the extent of the work involved by lending him or her this book. The partner should skim through it and read this chapter and the next one very carefully before deciding to pitch in.

Stop reading now, and go find yourself a partner. . . .

Got one? Good. Welcome back! Your partner's one long assignment is to read the passages *in italics*, which begin on page 54 and run through page 71, into a tape recorder. Don't read the instructions in between the italicized passages, just the passages themselves. Record each of the passages separately, leaving a comfortable space (ten seconds or so) between each one. Although a slow, careful reading should fill about sixty minutes of tape, do leave about three hours to complete the task. Your tapes should be as smooth and free of mistakes as possible, which means you may be doing a fair amount of stopping and starting, partner, if you're not prepared. Your best bet is to rehearse before your taping session by reading the passages all the way through two or three times.

This may sound like a lot of work, and it is. If your partner simply hasn't the time to do it, or if you haven't been able to find a partner, you may purchase my version of the taped exercises, which is available from Simon and Schuster.

But if a partner is ready and willing, it might be more effective to have the partner's voice on the tapes. The tapes will be the fearful flyer's primary tool for combatting flight fear, and they contain imaginary sequences that depict the presence of the partner in the airport and on the flight. If the voice you get used to hearing in these sequences is your partner's, having him or her with you for the real thing on flight day will be like a dream come true.

The content of the first tape passage, and an integral part of the other two is . . .

Breathing and Movement: This is the final portion of our Triple A/BM formula. As simple as this seems, breathing and movement are the two actions that can interrupt and moderate your rising anxiety. They constitute basic training for learning how to fly without fear. The breathing and movement techniques presented in the taped passages are relaxing, easy, and good for diminishing other sources of tension in your daily life, so spending time with them should be well worth it.

I inaugurated these exercises in my first seminar for fearful flyers. Even the most skeptical and stubborn participants ultimately recognized that they worked. They teach you a way to relax, and if you are relaxed, you will not be fearful. Fear and relaxation are opposite feeling states. Previously, you may have been distressed and threatened by clenched hands, dry throat, tight muscles, and a sense of impending doom. You can calm this seemingly uncontrollable fear and tension by learning how to relax controllable body responses. One benefit of this technique is its simplicity; a second is the amount of concentration practicing it requires. Since it's impossible for your mind to dwell on two things at once, just doing these exercises will help you to ignore your fears as you work to relax yourself.

Psychologists at the University of Houston who conducted a survey in one of our seminars there found that seminar participants considered the breathing and movement exercises the most important part of their preparation for fear-free flight. These exercises enabled them to intercept rising fear and tap an inner well of strength. Quite inexplicably, a new calm and courage surfaced that had been buried beneath overwhelming fear and doubt. Many said, "I expected to be fearful, but it never happened."

This approach to the treatment of tension and anxiety was first proposed about fifty years ago by a Dr. Edmund Jacobson. He correctly concluded that since muscle tension always went along with anxiety, conscious muscle relaxation might relieve anxiety. Unfortunately, his technique took over fifty sessions to learn. The techniques you will learn here will take one lesson to learn, although you will have to practice the simple procedures a number of times before you are comfortable and familiar with them.

Repetition is essential to the conditioning process. At the end of the first passage, you will be asked to listen to it again. Do so—if not right away, then soon after. Wait until you're completely at home with the material in the first passage before going on. Each time you listen, you will hear something new, and you will become more receptive, more hopeful of changing. These breathing and movement procedures are effective with any kind of anxiety or tension. Practice them and prove it to yourself!

Following the instructions for relaxation is a serious task, which requires your utmost attention. Let's assume that your partner has finished the tapes and that you are ready now to try them out.

First, choose to be alone in a quiet, comfortable place that is free from distractions. Unplug the phone. Settle into your favorite chair—preferably one with an armrest and a headrest. Later, you may choose to listen to these exercises lying down, but it is important that you are sitting up and alert for this initial learning session.

Get as comfortable as possible. Loosen any tight clothing, belts, or shoelaces. Sink easily and deeply into the chair. Put your full weight down. This suggestion may sound ridiculous, but the fearful flyer tries to sit on an airplane as lightly as possible, as if he were able to minimize the gravitational effect of his own weight. So practice putting your full weight down. Wiggle your buttocks into the seat. Shrug your shoulders up high and then let them drop. Do not cross your legs. Either rest them on a footstool or ottoman or put both feet flat on the floor. Place your hands in your lap, not touching each other.

Turn on your tape recorder.*

Partner: Your reading assignments are the italicized passages I, II, and III. Read them slowly and carefully.

PASSAGE I

For right now, decide that there is nothing else you need to attend to and direct your attention to my instructions. For the next few minutes, nudge aside all cares of the day or intruding thoughts. Please close your eyes to eliminate visual distractions. If something does occur that really requires your attention, your relaxed, subconscious mind will automatically make that determination. Like the sleeping mother who does not awaken to the hammering of housebuilders next door or the playful shouts of her children, but will, if she should hear just one distressful sound from her baby, become awake and alert quickly, be assured that you can become fully involved with these exercises without becoming isolated from your environment. Even your sleeping mind possesses a selective, innate vigilance.

This first exercise consists of slowly and sequentially taking three deep breaths, with my guidance during these learning stages. The idea is to ease into a comfortable and relaxed state. This exercise is our primary tool. All other procedures are related to the breathing exercise.

---

*WARNING: Do *not* listen to these tapes while driving. A few people go beyond relaxation while listening to these passages and become drowsy and sleepy. Drowsiness at the wheel of an automobile could be fatal.

Before I ask you to begin the breathing exercise, I want to explain why it is our primary tool in releasing you from your fear. Stress, excitement, and danger produce physiological responses that are involuntary—not directly controllable. Whether you are standing up to say two lines in a school play, or getting married, or boarding an airplane, or facing a firing squad, the responses are all similar: pounding heart, weakness, shortness of breath, pain in the pit of your stomach, tightness in the throat, cold hands, and so forth. All of these physical reactions are consequences of your emotional state, and only one can be directly and immediately controlled. Runaway anxiety can be intercepted and controlled by deliberately and consciously taking charge of your breathing. These deep breaths do not block or suppress the exaggerated feelings that threaten you. No. They divert those feelings, fragment them, and blunt them. They give you a sense of control. Taking charge of your breathing also moderates all those other involuntary reactions. You needn't ever feel helpless again!

You see, breathing is the very essence of our existence. Life, outside the womb, begins with our first breath—inspiration—and ends with our last breath—expiration. People who practice meditation or yoga recognize the importance of breathing exercises, not only for their benefits to health, insight, and discipline, but from a spiritual standpoint as well. So the next time you feel stressed, from any cause, use your natural, innate, and readily available remedy: breathe deeply of the energy of life.

Your benefits from these exercises are directly related to your decision to comply with the simple suggestions presented. Do not think of trying, for trying involves effort. Rather think of just going along—flowing, so to speak. After each inhalation, hold your breath for about three seconds before you exhale. This is about how long it takes to count slowly one thousand . . . two thousand . . . three thousand. Retaining the air for even that short a time will create a little bit of tension. This is planned that way because of the release you will receive as you exhale and let go of that tension. Think of that exhalation as letting off steam, releasing pressure—the pressure of tension and fear.

So comfortably settle into the seat and start now with the first of the three deep breaths. Inhale slowly and deeply. Hold that inhalation now as I count one thousand . . . two thousand . . . three thousand. Now exhale, let go, relax. Allow a refreshing passivity to come over you as you resume your normal breathing for a few moments.

Remember that there is a learning process involved here, and it may take you a few practice sessions to be able to respond easily and comfortably. Please be patient. Don't force the breaths. Slowly and deeply take that second breath, inhaling a little more fully this time. Hold that intake now for one thousand . . . two thousand . . . three thousand. Now exhale. Release that pressure. Let go. Exhale completely. Sink down a little further into the chair. Resume your normal manner of breathing.

Make the concluding breath of this exercise the fullest one yet. Inhale gently; really fill up. Good. Hold it for one thousand . . . two thousand . . . three thousand. Now let go of that pressure. Exhale. Relax. Feel loose, limp, lazy. Breathe normally. Being relaxed puts you in touch with the deeper level of your mind, where you can be free of stress and worry and fear. When you are calm and comfortable, you are at your best, physically and emotionally. Enjoy the peace that is available to you as we continue.

At this point, you have probably experienced a definite degree of comfort and passivity. However, there are some people who seem unable, at first, to accept a procedure for relaxing. When you begin to follow my suggestions and start to relax, you get a feeling of uneasiness. Just closing your eyes seems to be difficult. You have a pattern of always wanting to be in control. The thought of relaxing under my direction seems to threaten that control. It is difficult for you to let go, but do not be discouraged. Your response can be changed. Repetition, motivation, and familiarity all work to accomplish this. If you found that you were resisting the procedure, reverse the tape and start the exercise again. It's that simple.

Continue now to sit comfortably and easily as we do the second part of this introduction to progressive relaxation. Any distress or fear that you experience is always picked up and reflected in all the muscles of your body. Often it is retained for several hours. It may find an outlet as a headache, a backache, or a stomachache. Sickness may result. The word "disease" might be more accurately termed "dis-ease." Dis-ease creates fatigue, and fatigue is the most common complaint heard in the doctor's office. This part of the exercise is to detect and dispel muscle tension: dis-ease.

Check through your body now, starting from the top. Relax your scalp and your facial muscles. I trust that your eyelids have been and are now closed. Your jaw muscles pick up tension; avoid that by seeing that your lips are slightly parted, your teeth not clenched. The muscles of the neck and shoulders bear the brunt of a lot of anger, fear, and frustration. Relax those muscles now by shrugging the shoulders high and then dropping them down loose and limp. Continue to allow that loose and limp feeling to move down your arms and hands. Notice the weight of your arms and hands lying across your lap. Be loose. Be lazy. Make sure that the powerful long muscles of your thighs and the calves of your legs are relaxed. Be aware of how the weight of your legs can be felt through the bottoms of your feet, pressing down on the floor.

Let's go to the vital organs of the chest area, the heart and the lungs. The more you involve yourself in this procedure, the more your breathing will become easier and deeper, as in sleep. Your heart rate will slow as your heart muscle begins to pump more efficiently. With less resistance in your arteries, your blood pressure will also subside. Direct your attention to the internal muscles of your stomach and abdomen. Relax those muscles. They also reflect fear and tension states. You see, there is not one nerve, gland, or organ in your whole body that does not benefit as you loosen up, let go, and relax. A greater degree of calmness and relaxation may be obtained in this way than in a normal sleeping state, which can be restless and dream-disturbed.

Thus far, the purposes of these proceedings may seem rather vague to you. That's okay. It isn't even essential, at this point, that you believe that what we are doing will help you. It is essential, however, that you make a commitment to participate, to be attentive and receptive. The next exercise will relate more directly to the problem of your fear. That exercise will prepare you for the third exercise, which will train you to relax in the environment of a plane. Do not go on to the next exercise until you are very familiar and very comfortable with this one.

I'm going to count from one to ten now, in order that you may—if you wish—return to the full awareness of your immediate and familiar surroundings. Follow my suggestions as I count: one . . . two . . . Continue to feel comfortable and relaxed. And if there is a feeling of heaviness in any part of your body, let it fade away. Three . . . four . . . The changes that you seek are occurring at the deeper, relaxed levels of your mind. Five . . . six . . . When you are ready, open your eyes. Seven . . . eight . . . Be patient; be hopeful. Feel good about your decision to free yourself from the restrictions imposed by your fear. Nine . . . ten . . . Be renewed in energy and in spirit. And when you are ready—and if you choose—slowly and easily stand up and stretch.

Make sure you listen to Passage I a number of times before you move on to . . .

PASSAGE II

Now we're going to deal with the threatening feelings you've had in the past. Either going on the flight or turning away from it has embarrassed you, to say the least, or—in a more severe form—has caused you to feel that you would faint, scream, panic, or even die. That vivid memory can only be dispelled by being confronted. Ignoring or suppressing those feelings only magnifies them. If we are going to coax your fear down the stairs, those past demons must be neutralized before we can go on to programming a new response. Let's see what happened to cause your misery.

To get to this sore spot requires that you again go to a deep level of relaxation. First, relax by gently moving your legs from side to side. Shift your weight, your derrière. Slowly rotate and shrug your shoulders. Move your hands and head. To conserve time, I'm not going to direct you precisely in taking the three deep breaths but ask you that you do them on your own, slowly and easily. Remember to hold each inhalation for the count of one thousand . . . two thousand . . . three thousand . . . before exhaling and letting off some of the pressure that may build up as we explore these sensitive areas. Complete the exercise as I continue.

The undesirable thoughts of flying can be diffused by reviewing your past experience. Do this as an observer to avoid reinvolving yourself emotionally. Prepare to observe yourself with a sense of detachment, as if the unpleasantness had been filmed and you have asked for a rerun. Start the film at the point where the tension started building. Was it two weeks before the flight or one day? Were you at the airport waiting in the boarding lounge? Calmly observe how you created your misery. Were you alone? Did you talk to someone? What did you say? Did you feel conspicuous? Frustrated? Helpless? Desperate? Were you hurting? If at this point you turned back, examine the consequent feelings of relief . . . and regret. If you boarded and hung in there for the takeoff, recall some of the anxieties.

Did this so-called film depict the tension that must have been expressed in your face, in your hands, in the rigidity of your body posture? Didn't your feelings moderate during some part of the flight? How did it go during the landing? Note that even now there is a tendency to hold your breath as you recall that distress. Breathe deeply. Were you disturbed by what the plane seemed to be doing, or by what you seemed to be doing?

Did you try to avoid the reality of the flight experience by sitting rigidly, holding on, looking neither right nor left, or by closing your eyes? Did that—or anything that you did—help? In looking back, weren't you more frightened by what you imagined might happen than with what was actually happening? Weren't your fears caused by your runaway imagination? Weren't you obsessively focusing on problems of "What if I scream?" "What if I faint?" "What if I embarrass myself?" No wonder you suffered.

At first, recalling those fears may be stressful. The stress will lessen each time you listen to this exercise. If, however, you again become very frightened, stop the exercise and regain your composure by shifting your attention to the deep breathing routine. This procedure will serve well to counter your distress. Familiarity should gradually blunt the effect of your past torments.

Participate in these exercises. Listen. Feel. Follow directions. Go with it. Drop some of those old concepts that haven't worked. Tune in to these concepts that will work. These exercises are not easy. Change is difficult. Your progress may seem very slow, but we are just beginning. Right now it is enough to stem the tide of your fear and give you hope. I suggest that you listen several times to this exercise and the one before it, before going on to exercise three.

If you now wish to return to a full awareness of your immediate surroundings, follow my suggestions as I count from one to ten. One . . . two . . . Continue to feel comfortable and relaxed, but let any feelings of heaviness in your body fade away. Three . . . four . . . The changes that you seek are occurring at the deeper, more relaxed levels of your mind. Five . . . six . . . When you are ready, open your eyes. Seven . . .

eight . . . Be hopeful; be patient. Nine . . . ten . . . Be renewed in energy and spirit. And if you choose and when you are ready, slowly and easily stand up and stretch.

PASSAGE III

Part of that last exercise may have shaken you up a bit. I hope so. The more shook up, the less cover-up. Covering up, to avoid looking honestly and insightfully at your feelings, means keeping them. Most fearful flyers wish to overcome their fear, but very few are willing to risk changing, or even examining the risk of changing. Einstein said that imagination is more powerful than knowledge. Without imagination, without dreams or hopes or even fantasies, our lives would be barren. So work hard with this next exercise as we take an imaginary flight.

Position yourself again in a quiet, comfortable place where you will be alone. Do the deep breathing exercise on your own as I deepen your relaxation by counting from ten to one: ten . . . nine . . . Close your eyes, sit back, relax, and let go of control. Eight . . . seven . . . Check through the muscles of your body. If you detect an area that is tight or tense, permit that grip to be released as I continue counting. Six . . . five . . . Allow yourself to become as loose and limp as an old rag doll. Four . . . three . . . Permit a feeling of passivity to flow in. Two . . . one . . . Relax completely.

Just closing your eyes puts you in touch with your subconscious. You are in touch with that wondrous part of your mind whenever you do anything that holds your attention, such as watching a film or reading an interest-

ing book, recalling a pleasant experience, or listening to soaring music. Your relaxed, subconscious mind is receptive, creative, and very imaginative. Your irrational fear is a consequence of your creative imagination used adversely. Now we want to use that powerful creative force to process and program a new, acceptable, and tolerable response. If you will vividly imagine the flight we are about to experience, it will be recorded and impressed in your mind as actually taking place. Fantasy and reality will then merge as one.

Visualize meeting me at the airport for a flight to a city of your choice. Let's suppose that our reservations have been made and that we have our tickets in hand. Without luggage we can proceed to the departure gate. A departure display board or screen near the airline's ticket counter will give us the gate number and location.

Now I know that you feel shaky, that your throat may be dry, your stomach protesting, and your heart rate accelerated. All these symptoms are characteristic of a low to moderate anxiety state. Accept those feelings. Accept also a feeling of excitement! You have had similar feelings on the occasion of your first date, your first job interview, or any of a dozen exciting events in your life. Accept those feelings, and they will subside. Resist them, and they will persist.

Let's proceed by moving toward our goal just one step at a time. Instead of projecting problems, let us confront just one obstacle at a time. We are coming up now on the security area. As soon as we pass through this routine check, we will find a place to sit down and use some of our coping tools. If you have a purse or package, you will be asked to place it on the conveyor belt that moves it through an X-ray–like screening device. We then walk under a metal-detecting archway. No problem here.

Now let's sit down for a minute to regain our strength and assess your progress. We have been wise in planning ample time for these rest stops. Sit all the way back in your seat—not on the edge—and slowly take a couple of really deep breaths, exhaling with sighs of relief and release. At this point, tears may flow. Let them come. Tears represent a very encouraging breakthrough, especially for men. Your tears are not tears of sadness, but tears of aliveness, humanness, and sensitivity. They have a healing quality. People in your past who told you not to cry meant well, but they were telling you to cover up your feelings. You've covered up long enough. Now open up.

Let's move on to the departure lounge and select our seats. We will sit toward the front, where it's smoother and quieter. Before they announce that our flight is ready for boarding, I would like you to recognize that right now, at this moment, you are doing okay—even though you are nervous and excited. You are handling the present. Neither you nor anyone else can handle the future. Your difficulty comes from your dreadful and implausible anticipations. Instead of dwelling on dire and foreboding projections, choose to dwell on the reality of the here and now. The deep breathing keeps your attention in the present.

They have announced our flight, and I will explain the other major coping tool as we line up to enter the aircraft. Breathing is a now activity and so is movement. Voluntary movement loosens muscles that have involuntarily tightened from fear. This movement can be done sitting or standing. We will rehearse now, standing, so that you can do them later, sitting on the plane. Slowly and gently move your head in a circle a couple of times. Shrug your shoulders high, inhaling as you do so.

Exhale completely as you let them drop. Extend your arms sideways and then forward, briskly. Shift your weight from one foot to the other at a pace equivalent to a fast walk, or simply move your feet up and down as if you were marking time. If doing all of this makes you feel conspicuous, that's all right. Feel conspicuous, and let it serve to distract you from your fear.

Ordinarily after boarding, I ask you to take a peek in the cockpit, but on this flight let's move along to the seats that the flight attendant has indicated. Look around. Notice the colors of the interior of the plane, the windowed side walls, the overhead storage compartments. Notice also the other passengers moving about, chatting, settling into their seats. Settle all the way into yours now as the entrance door is being closed.

This is also a very appropriate time to again go through the breathing and movement exercises. Do it whether you think you need it or not. Do it without my cue. Do it because it will bridle your anxiety.

The cabin attendants will begin making announcements now, asking that you fasten your seat belt and demonstrating the use of the oxygen masks and the life vests. Government regulations require this. The primary responsibility of the flight crew and the cabin attendants is your safety.

Note the sound of the engines as they start and the big compressors spin up and come alive with power. Hear the sound now. The cabin lights may flicker as electrical power is changed over from an outside source to the aircraft engine's generators. The aircraft is pushed back from the boarding gate by a large, low tug attached to the nose wheel.

Haven't your feelings been mixed? Aren't they difficult to label as anxiety or stress or excitement or fear? All

65

of those feelings are transitory and variable in intensity. Let me assure you that they will not overwhelm you or incapacitate you or embarrass you or demean you. As we taxi, think of the airplane as a big and graceful bird that feels out of place on the ground. It protests by thumping and squeaking and sometimes lurching about. Each kind of plane has its own kind of grunts and groans. Sounds will vary according to where you are seated. Your concern about those sounds will gradually diminish.

The cockpit crew have now completed their thorough checklist, and as we move onto the end of the runway, I want you to get ready to wiggle your toes. That's right! Wiggling your toes during takeoff keeps you occupied. It's fun! And it really works. Let's hold hands also. So lean way back in your seat, breathe deeply, keep your eyes open. Note the steadily increasing roar of jet engine power as the pilot advances the throttles, and wiggle your toes. As we accelerate, move those toes faster and faster. The takeoff run usually lasts between thirty and fifty seconds depending on the size of the aircraft. Now the nose is coming up, and we are flying off with a sharp, clean break from Earth. The angle of climb may seem sharp to you, but it is normal—about fifteen degrees. How about letting go with a big sigh of relief? Both you and the plane have miraculously managed to become airborne, and neither of you has come apart. I congratulate you!

The after-takeoff sound that may have disturbed you in the past is caused by the retraction of the landing gear. First, doors on the underbelly of the plane open up so that the wheels of the plane can be brought up and stored. Then the doors are closed. Listen to those sounds every time you fly. They occur a few seconds after takeoff. After that, you will hear a bell as the no-smoking sign is turned off.

If this first turn seems uncomfortably steep to you, let me explain to you that from the cabin of all our jet transports you are looking down at the wings. From this perspective the bank seems steeper than it actually is. But especially note that none of these things is bothering you nearly as much as you had anticipated. You are making progress.

Now the pilot is reducing power on the engines. This reduces our engine's noise. At the same time he has reduced our angle of takeoff climb. Previously, this may have been a frightening sensation for you because this reduction of power and simultaneous decrease of climb angle changes the gravitational field. You may momentarily feel lighter in your seat.

Look out the window. This may be difficult for you, but it is just another one of the minor blocks that threaten you because you've avoided confronting it. At first, just take a quick look, just a peek, a glance. Later, extend that glance to five seconds. Then ten, or twenty, or more. You can do it. Soon, much to your satisfaction and pleasure, you will become engrossed with cloud shapes and the panorama below. Look out the window to see if you can see the flaps extended on the rear edge of the wing. They give us extra lift for the takeoff. When they are later retracted into the wings, the flight will become smoother, more streamlined.

As soon as that seatbelt sign goes off, I want you to stand up and stretch. You needn't move out of your seat and into the aisle just yet, unless you feel like it. But move your arms and legs up and down like a soldier marching in place. Turn your body both ways. Tension always settles into muscles. Physical movement will dissipate it.

Now, imagine that we have climbed to our assigned cruising altitude of 35,000 feet—almost seven miles above the Earth. It's beautiful! The flight attendants are serving refreshments, and right now it is as smooth as if you were sitting in your own living room. I have made many ocean crossings that were smooth like this all the way over and all the way back.

This flight, however, will not continue to be as smooth as cutting butter because the captain has just announced that he is putting the seatbelt sign back on. Some choppiness has been reported in the area up ahead. I know that turbulence has been a particular concern of yours, and so I am glad that I can guide you through the experience. No matter how rough the weather might be, remember that it is not a hazard to the structure of this aircraft. It is built as strong as a battleship. It is stable, too. The ride can be bumpy, but planes do not fall or tip over.

Now, as we are entering choppy air, note that the wings seem to be waving at us. They are not rigid. Their strength is in their flexibility. They are designed and extensively tested so that, at their tips, they can flex at least eight feet above and below their center line, like a giant bird. The aircraft eases itself over this rough road like it was riding on huge, cushioned springs. Remember that it is moving through its own element—air. There are no air pockets. Air has substance, density, weight, and movement. Air supports this plane as a boat is supported as it moves across the water's surface. The fact is, air is a smoother medium for travel than surface transportation and much less hazardous. One former

*fearful flyer says, "Now, when the road in the air
becomes rough, I imagine I am riding in a royal carriage
bouncing over a cobblestone road in jolly old England."*

Once you have learned to relax in flight, you will be
able to move with the airplane, turn with it, and become
a part of it. It is your resistance to that movement, your
holding on, that creates the problem. Keep those muscles
loose because taking the strain off your body also takes
the strain off your mind. It works both ways. Shrug!
Bend! Wiggle! Turn! Move!

Well, as often happens, that choppiness has only
lasted a few minutes, and now we are on a smooth road
again. The captain has turned the seatbelt sign off. I
know that you have been through quite a bit today, but I
want you to take another step. Literally, I want you to
step out into the aisle, and slowly, with determination,
move toward one of the toilets. It might not be easy;
most of these confrontations aren't. You needn't hurry.
Stop halfway and do some deep breathing if you feel you
need it. Or you can benefit from the distraction of
talking to a stranger. Risk it!

When you finally get to the toilet entrance, pause to
congratulate yourself on your progress. Then step inside. If you only stay in for three seconds with the door
open, that's okay. Next time, stay for ten seconds. Set up
your own plan for desensitization. What you are really
aiming for is to be able to go inside, lock the door, and
stay at least long enough to wash your hands. If locking
that door seems stressful to you now, then review and
vividly visualize each step until familiarity dulls the
sting.

The captain has just announced that we will be
starting our descent very soon. Imagine that we will be
landing in the place you hope to fly to. Sometimes you

can hear the reduction in engine power. As in an automobile, when you start down a hill, you ease off on the accelerator. Most pilots ease into the descent, so that you are scarcely aware of it. However, a few pilots may start a descent with an abruptness that might get your attention. Descent may begin as far as 200 miles out and take more than thirty minutes.

About midway through our descent, the pilot will likely be using the airbrakes, or spoilers. They slow the plane down, and their use may result in a mild but steady vibration. Sometimes you can see those airbrakes extended on top of the wing. After they are retracted, it will be smooth again for a few minutes, until the wing flaps are extended. Again you will feel a slight, steady vibration. They are extended to slow the aircraft for the approach and for the landing.

Although it is cloudy and raining outside, be assured that if the weather at the airport should worsen—something which is very unlikely—there is plenty of fuel still available to take us to a choice of other airports. Next in sequence is the lowering of the landing gear. You may notice the airplane shake a little as that heavy gear extends and the wheels lock firmly in place. The flight attendants are moving into their assigned seats. The pilots are guided to the runway by several confirming and reliable instruments in the cockpit. They can land easily and safely in weather conditions unsafe for driving.

Now, as we descend through the cloud layer, you can see the ground. As we land smoothly, be prepared for a loud roar when the flow of thrust of our jet engines is reversed, directing our engine exhaust power forward instead of rearward and aiding us in slowing down. The resulting noise, however, seems to exceed that of takeoff.

This flight has been a short one, but it affords excellent practice. You need all the practice you can get. Although this trip was an exercise of your imagination, your subconscious mind doesn't differentiate between the real and the imagined. It records and stores feelings and responses as a flight experience.

Now, if you choose to return to the reality of your environment, follow my instructions as I count from one through ten. One . . . two . . . Rouse yourself slowly and gently. Three . . . four . . . Open your eyes when you are ready. Five . . . six . . . Be relaxed and at ease. Seven . . . eight . . . Be patient but persistent in your effort to displace your fear with faith—faith in yourself. Nine . . . ten . . . Feel good about yourself. And if you wish, gently stand and stretch.

NOTE: If the suggestions or procedures in these passages persistently upset you, do seek the counsel and guidance of a psychologist. Usually the individual treatment of phobias is relatively short-term and successful.

CHAPTER III

PLANNING YOUR NEXT FLIGHT

> You gain strength, courage and confidence by every experience in which you really stop to look fear in the face . . . You must do the thing you think you cannot do.
>
> —Eleanor Roosevelt

IF YOU HAVE PRACTICED THE EXERCISES, AND IF YOU'RE *really* tired of being afraid, you are now ready to confront your fear of flying. Up until now, you've been given "book learning"—useful, comforting, but distant. In this chapter you are going to complete the work of freeing yourself from your fears.

The truth of any situation in life cannot be given or transferred. Truth can only be experienced. The fundamental experience of overcoming your fear is flight itself. Instead of experiencing flying distortedly and unrealistically—as you have done before—you can get in touch with what really happens. As Werner Erhard has said, "A fear completely experienced disappears."

The concepts presented by Triple A/BM are a simplification, an overview. The process of using those tools in flight is an adventure that will enhance your self-esteem and allow you to recognize your ability to change and to grow. The only thing you have to lose is fear.

Your first task is to go over the exercises again until you are thoroughly acquainted with them. We recommend that you listen to them five times over a period of two weeks or ten times over a month before you fly. Each time you listen, set aside an hour or so for yourself and run them all the way through. Take them seriously. This may seem like a lot of listening, and there will be times when you will want to be done with all of this "dress rehearsal," but be patient. Each time you go through the tapes, you will be imprinting their valuable information and suggestions more deeply in your mind. They're like emotional insurance. Thousands of people have proved them effective in combatting fear and anxiety. Don't worry that you will be bored by them. Former fearful flyers say that they hear something new every time they listen to them.

Just listening is not quite enough. You must involve your imagination in the process, tune in to the information, accept the premise that if you are relaxed, you cannot be afraid. The ideas are not hypothetical: they have evolved from experience, and they are tailor-made for fearful flyers. The simulated flight will come through as a real experience if you let go, relax, and flow with it.

One way or another you have worked out some way to accommodate your fear of flying. A part of you has bowed before this fear that limits your life, your travel, your vacations, your visits to friends and relations, your access to the convenience and safety of jet transportation. Your fear is strong, pervasive, and used to being in charge. A part of you is put down by the persistent burden of your fear. This part of you I call the "left side." (No offense to southpaws; this is just a convenient metaphor.)

There is another part of you I call the "right side." The right side says, "I really want to change." Your right side is sick and tired of being daunted by your fear; it wants to throw the weight off your back. It wants you to be free, unencumbered by the limitations your fear has created. The right side knows very well that something should be done. It is the side that says, "Yes, I'm frightened, but I'm going to try to do it, even if I feel I might fail."

Your right side is also the side that makes you feel good about yourself. The right side is unlimited in its possibilities. Every good thought that you have ever had, whether it be one of caring about someone else or caring about yourself, or accomplishing something, comes from your right side.

Your left side, on the other hand, is the unhappy side, the limited side. The left side of you is mired in the mud of your negative thinking. The left side is the one that makes you feel helpless and hopeless. The left side doesn't move. It's the dead side of you. It's the side that dwells in the past and upon negative experiences. The left side anticipates dire possibilities, saying, "What if, what if . . .?"

Whereas the left side will always tell you, "I can't do it," the right side will say, more honestly, "I won't do it." Keep in mind that all of us have our left side and our right side. But only you can determine which one you are going to listen to, which one you're going to allow to run your life.

As you listen to the tapes, as you begin to consider the possibility of a comfortable flight, your left and right sides will stage daily battles for your will. Learn to distinguish your left side from your right side. Learn to pause and question whatever your left side tells you. Learn to be more open to your right side, instead, which will continue to grow stronger as you listen to it.

Get a piece of paper and draw a line down the center of it. Take a pencil and label the top left side "Avoidances." Under it list the various ways in which you have avoided the experience of flight, either as a fearful flyer or a fearful nonflyer. Be honest now. You *have* resisted flying; write down how you did it. Label the top right half of the paper "Small Changes." Under this heading, jot down some slight changes that you can make today. For instance, if one of your avoidances was to drive out of your way to avoid an airport, decide to drive within five miles of one, or four miles, or up to one of the perimeter roads and back out again. If you have avoided looking up at airplanes, or out of them when you are aboard, resolve to take a quick peek next time. Make these small goals feasible. Write them down. Have some achievable plan for all the avoidances you listed.

Okay, you've "listened" up to here, and you're ready for the next step. Which means you're ready to organize yourself for your first flight.

Keep in mind, as you follow the guidelines I will give you, that this flight will be a new experience; you will be flying in a completely different manner than you have flown before. Now, at last, you will have the tools to deal with yourself on a plane. There will be some fear that comes up, but it will also recede. Someone once told me that his fear came in waves, but it also receded in waves. It shows up, hangs around for a moment or two, and then dissipates.

In particular, don't worry that your fear will make you lose control of yourself. A clinical psychologist from Sweden wrote to me several years ago asking if he might come to the United States and attend one of our seminars as a student of my methods. I wrote back to say that I would be pleased to have him visit us, and he came to Dallas for a large seminar there. He was a very likable young man but quite shy because he felt that his English was inadequate. With my encouragement he finally agreed to give us some of his observations. (Most of the phobics he worked with had trouble traveling on buses or streetcars. Public transportation is widely used in Sweden.)

He drew a diagonal line on the blackboard from the lower left-hand corner to the upper right-hand corner. The lower corner he labeled with a zero, the top corner with a ten. He asked us to let zero represent the absence of anxiety and ten represent madness, disorientation, the complete loss of control. He then drew a couple of intersecting lines at mid-level. He said that most of the people he had worked with were afraid of losing control as a consequence of their mounting terror at being closed in. Some, he said, would give up and get off when they got to the uncomfortable level of a four or five. Maybe they were perspiring, maybe they felt a tightness in their throat or stomach, had weak knees, and were afraid that they might lose control at any time.

His reassuring message was that those who stayed on and confronted their fright *did not ever go beyond a five level*. My experience confirms the fact that the symptoms anticipated by fearful flyers far exceed those actually experienced in flight. Furthermore, the anxiety level reduces after takeoff.

So many of the people in my first seminars were convinced that they would go berserk once they were "trapped" in the airplane that I requested several first-rate therapists to address the validity of that threat. I learned that a phobic person's anxiety is vastly and categorically different from the break with reality and the personality disorganization of someone who is psychotic. An episode of madness does not suddenly erupt in someone who is seeking help and guidance.

Now that you know that you aren't going to lose it when you fly, do yourself a favor and ease up on yourself when feelings of fear arise. As I have said repeatedly, one of the biggest problems confronting phobics of any kind is their insistence on being in control. You will continue to keep your fears until you allow yourself to be imperfect and hurt a little bit. Give yourself permission *not* to be in total control of yourself. By giving up control and allowing those feelings to surface, you will alleviate your anxiety and find yourself at a manageable level.

If you're unwilling to experience being afraid, you will continue to be afraid, but if you're willing to be afraid, you are en route to being fearless. Be realistic. Expect to be nervous. Be human, feeling, real, yourself —gloriously imperfect. At times we are all brave and cowardly, wise and foolish, generous and stingy, fearful and fearless. Remember what you've learned in the

77

exercises. Accept your feelings of fear, knowing that you have learned how to moderate and reduce them.

Now, let's fly!

Work out a comfortable schedule with your partner that encompasses the following guidelines in their approximate order.

1. Visit airports. Somewhere on the periphery of all airports is a vantage point from which you can watch the planes take off and land. If ten minutes of this is all you can handle, note that the next time you'll be able to handle fifteen minutes. Keep it up.

2. Ask your friend to visit the departure area of the airport with you. If you begin to feel like turning back, stop and do the breathing and movement exercises. Exaggerate the movements—shake, bend, and wiggle!

3. Call or visit the passenger service manager of an airline. Tell the service manager you're fearful about flying and ask for permission to board a parked aircraft for ten minutes. Sit down in the roomy first-class section. Accept any anxiety this might provoke and do the breathing and movement exercises. On your next visit, select a different airline, and this time spend your time walking around the cabin, looking, touching, and exploring. Ask as many questions as you want about the number of seats, safety procedures, etc.

(Note: All airlines employ people whose job it is to look after requests such as yours. Almost everyone you encounter on these visits will be helpful and understanding. If by some chance you get a lemon, don't let that person bluff you into thinking you're weird for seeking such assistance. Choose another airline. If a company isn't interested in attracting new business, there's no reason to give it yours.)

4. Recognize, during these visits, that your phobic habit is to avoid confrontation by retreating. Recognize also that stepping back on only one of three confrontations still leaves you two steps ahead. Be persistent, but avoid trying to be perfect.

5. Avoid swapping stories with other fearful flyers. Their exaggerations and distortions are contagious.

6. This is a biggie. Plan a short flight to a nearby city, preferably one where some friends will be waiting for you or one that you've always wanted to visit. This is your "graduation flight"—the completion of your course in overcoming the fear of flying. It is the first of many flights, which will become increasingly comfortable for you.

   Book two seats, the second one for your partner. Try to find a morning flight so you'll have less time to worry between waking up and taking off. Book at the airport at a relatively quiet time so that you can ask as many questions about the flight as you wish without feeling harried or rushed. Fly first class, if it makes you feel more comfortable, but any seat closer to the front of the airplane will be smoother and quieter.

   If the airline offers to reserve seat assignments at the same time that you book your reservations, take them up on it. Ask the ticket agent what kind of plane will take you to your destination; then go look at one like it so that you'll know what to expect.

Expect, when making the reservation, to feel nervous and perhaps reluctant. This is a big step, after all. You're committing yourself to flying, and your "what if" mechanism is bound to kick into gear, if only at half speed. Remember that the stress that you feel may come from your reluctance to give up your problem. One seminar participant told me that her fear of flying always brought her attention and compassion from her family and friends. It was hard for her to give up all of that, but her urge to fly won out in the end. Remember also that your emotions will continue to ride on their own roller coaster from now until the flight. Go along for the ride. For as many downs as you experience, there will be ups as well. Be patient with yourself!

7. During the period between booking your flight and flying, continue to listen to the tapes (now they'll be second nature to you, like an old friend). Visit the airport again if you feel you need to. Confide your hopes and fears to your partner, but try not to dwell on them. At this point some people get a little superstitious. ("I thought about crashing today: does that mean my flight is going to crash?" "I felt fine yesterday, but today I'm a little nervous. What if it gets worse and worse?") The fact of the matter is that *nothing* that happens on the day you fly will be *anything* like you thought it would be. The gap between the present and the future is unimaginable in your circumstances. No matter what you think or how you feel right now,

your flight will be an experience entirely unto itself.

8. The night before your graduation flight, get yourself entirely organized, so that you'll have no logistics to bother you in the morning. Pack your bag, double-check your tickets, and go to an early movie or out to dinner with friends or family. At some point before you retire, listen to the tapes once more. It will help you get a good night's sleep.

   If you don't sleep perfectly soundly, don't worry about it. Read a book or watch a late-night movie. Most people who take the seminar or read this book are surprised at how well they do sleep the night before their "maiden voyage." But even if you sleep fitfully, it will make little difference. Our bodies get the rest they need according to their circumstances, and you can be assured that, no matter what, you will be physically, as well as emotionally, prepared for the morning.

9. On the day of your graduation flight, take it easy on the coffee and sugary foods, both of which have a tendency to jazz you up. Give yourself plenty of time to get to the airport an hour before your flight. If you don't have an advance seat assignment, choose those seats up front when you get to the ticket counter.

   Talk to your partner about how you're feeling. Whenever you get the urge to turn back, stop—but don't go back. Instead, concentrate on the deep breathing and movement exercises. Whenever your left side begins to say, "What if (I cry, I go crazy, there's turbulence)?", let your right side substitute

"So what if?" Allow yourself those dire forebodings, and then put a "so what?" in front of them. Express your fear as anger, get mad at the plane—it's a simpler reaction.

Listen to that voice (maybe it's only a whisper) that brought you here. If you feel like crying, cry. Don't try to figure out why, just let the tears flow. You'll feel better. Those tears may represent long-repressed feelings that need release. Men in our classes often tell me that their "breakthrough"—the moment when they knew they could do it—came when they finally allowed themselves to cry.

10. One way to avoid obsessively focusing on your fear—one so effective it deserves separate mention—is to stop at the airport newsstand and buy a startling pictorial magazine like *Playboy* or *Playgirl*. The pictures will probably revolt or intrigue you. Either reaction is preferable to fear.

11. Choose to give some attention to what is happening around you. Aren't there playful children nearby, or a sleeping infant, or a romantic couple swapping glances? Speak to a stranger.

12. After you arrive in the boarding lounge, find a quiet place to do your breathing exercises. Take the cassette tapes along to guide you. It's fine to bring your tape recorder on board. If you catch yourself dwelling on the reasons why you may not make the flight, give at least equal time to reasons why you can succeed, and why you want to. Accept your nervousness and note that it varies. Aren't you also excited? If the wait in the departure lounge seems unbearably long, sneak a look at "them dirty

pictures." The point is not to "get a grip on yourself"; it is to float.

Your thoughts and feelings of fear may be *uncomfortable*, but they are *not dangerous*. If you allow them to surface and then you function in spite of them, they will fade. Remember, don't try to get rid of the feelings. You have a reliable nervous system that can take care of itself. Expect to be nervous, excited, and uneasy. Accept all of those feelings. Big events like getting a new job, getting married, having a baby, leaving home, being stopped by a traffic cop, all make you feel this way. Breathing is the primary antidote for fear. Movement is second: stand, stretch, wiggle, shrug, shake, bend—anything that works for you.

13. *Pinpoint your anxiety on a scale of 0 to 10.* Zero means no anxious feelings or thoughts. Ten means the feelings and thoughts are so intense that you think you must leave. *Monitor your levels; don't judge them.* Watch your anxiety go up and down. The level of your fear changes with your concentration. *Your level will come down if you stay in the present. It will increase if you plan your escape or try to get rid of your feelings.* If you watch the levels change, you will be pleasantly surprised to find how seldom really high levels occur and how briefly they last.

Remain in the present. Try not to go off into the past or the future. Don't talk to yourself in *"what if's"* but in *"but before's."* For example, instead of thinking, *"What if* everything gets worse and I die or go crazy?" think, "I feel okay, *but before* when I was here, I thought I was going to panic."

Try to locate the tension in your body. Are you holding your shoulders up, craning your neck forward, clenching your teeth or your fists? See if you can make the tension greater, then relax.

14. As you come on board, tell the flight attendant that you are a fearful flyer and that you would like to take one little peek into the cockpit. I've never heard of anyone being denied this privilege. Introduce yourself to the crew members.

15. After you've taken your seat and fastened your seat belt, there is still a lot of body movement you can do. Do it! It is so important. Take some deep breaths. You can still find space to move your arms and legs. Wiggle your buttocks down into the seat and lean forward and back. Explain your procedures to your neighbors by simply saying that this is a procedure recommended for anxious flyers. If you're embarrassed, be so. It beats being afraid. *Act* more than *react*. Cry. Yawn. Joke. Smile at a baby. Follow the emergency procedure demonstrations.

16. Be aware that you are no longer helpless and that you now have coping tools. Being fearful is nothing to be ashamed of; admit it, let it show, and deal with it. Listen for the start-up of the engines, observe the flicker of the lights as the electrical system switches from the auxiliary power unit to the power of the engines themselves.

17. Take two deep breaths as the plane is lined up for takeoff. Lean back in your seat. Do not grip anything or close your eyes. As the plane accelerates down the runway, wiggle your toes. Faster as

you accelerate. It helps! The takeoff run takes thirty to fifty seconds. Time it.

18. After lift-off, listen for the sound of the landing gear being retracted and the ring of the bell that signals that the no-smoking sign is off. Stay with the moment. You can handle this. It's your dire projections that threaten you and disturb you. In all the people I have worked with, the fear of heights and of being closed in seems to dissipate quite easily once the flight is under way. As a way of putting your new tools to good use, try to use this opportunity to practice and improve your skills rather than follow your old anxious, anticipatory way. Practice; don't test yourself.

   Fighting to get complete control equals tension. Define your job. Don't try to manage the whole world. To do so will only increase your tension and confusion. You don't have to fly the plane; that's not your job. As a passenger, your job is to sit and ride. That's all you have to do, as comfortably as you can.

19. Look around you. Look outside. Just a glance at first. Gradually extend your glance to a long peek. Persist. Go with the movement of the plane; don't anticipate or resist it. You are part of it now. If you still feel a little tense, wiggle your buttocks, legs, and arms.

20. As soon as the seatbelt light is turned off, stand up, stretch, move about, and rejoice. Go to the washroom, even just to close the door and wash your hands. Explore the plane. Find someone who appears to be nervous and offer to share your

experience with him. Congratulate yourself. Someone said, "The greatest victory of all is the victory over one's self." Thousands of former fearful flyers say that their "maiden voyage" was the most triumphant experience of their lives.

21. Your triumph over fear will be enhanced with each flight. After you've "survived" your graduation flight, survive another as soon as you can, within two weeks if possible. Note how much more survivable that one is. It is very important to affirm the experience. People say things like, "I can't believe I did it!" "I looked out the window for the first time ever!" "I got out of my seat!" Keep flying until all your unwanted responses have subsided. Take the momentum. Do the exercises. Don't assume you don't need them. Prove to yourself that it's as easy as you hoped it would be.

If, for some reason, you don't end up getting on—or staying on—the plane the first time, *take it easy on yourself!* This is not a final exam, or a job interview, or a beauty pageant. You're doing something for *yourself,* and the only standards of success that apply are your own.

Approximately 10 percent of the people who attend our seminars drop out before the graduation flight. They aren't failures; they only missed an opportunity that day. Many try again and succeed. If this happens to you the first time around, remember that you are not noticeably different from those who do fly the first time. There is a very thin line between staying on and turning back. It's like diving off the high board the first time. The left-sided you tugs at you to turn back. The right-sided you urges you to hang in there. The difference will be in which one you choose to listen to.

If you find yourself saying, "I can't make the trip," tell yourself, "I have *decided* not to take *this* trip." The latter is a conscious choice. Courage is seldom based on bravery, guts, or heroism. It's based on a choice of alternatives. So today you didn't choose to go. Next time you can choose differently. Talk to yourself about what you did right! You practiced. You made a reservation. You came to the airport. You're doing fine. Keep it up, and try again soon.

Occasionally a fearful flyer will tell me that his or her first flight "wasn't as good as I hoped it would be." If you find yourself trying to fine-tune your flying experiences, you're being a perfectionist. Lower your expectations. Many nonfearful flyers feel uncomfortable occasionally, if only because they're feeling out of sorts anyway, or because the ride is a little bumpy. Join the crowd! Don't make too much of the little things. You are flying. That in itself is a miracle for you.

CHAPTER IV

FLYING TODAY

I HAVE STRESSED THROUGHOUT THIS BOOK THAT YOUR FEAR of flying is irrational—that flying poses no danger that would ever justify your fearful reactions. Now I'm going to explain how and why flying today is a very un-risky enterprise.

How safe is flying? There are so many ways to answer the question! The short answer, and least helpful because it's so abstract, is that flying on a U.S. scheduled airline is 99.99998 percent safe. According to Robert J. Serling, noted aviation writer, this figure "compares most favorably with virtually any form of human activity, including taking a bath." (The term "U.S. scheduled airlines" denotes what we normally think of when we "take a plane" somewhere. It includes all of the "household name" airlines—Eastern, Pan Am, United, etc.—which usually use larger jet transports, from DC-9s to 747s. These scheduled flights carry 95 percent of all passengers on air transportation in the U.S.)

Taking a plane is significantly safer than using electrical power (the kind you plug your TV into), or swimming, surgery, X-rays, large construction, hunting, home appliances, and contraceptives (from a report published by Decision Research [a subsidiary of Perceptronics, Inc.] in 1979).

But what does 99.99998 percent really mean? "Not 100 percent" is what a fearful flyer would say, so why don't we look at other figures to put this big one into perspective. During the five years from 1981 through 1985, the U.S. scheduled airlines flew *1.6 billion passengers through 26 million takeoffs and landings* with an average fatality rate of ninety per year. 1981 and 1984 saw only four fatalities each. For the purpose of comparison, let's look at flying versus other modes of transportation.

In 1985, there were 48,400 transportation fatalities in the U.S. Of these, 22,800 were in passenger cars, 7,800 were pedestrians, 6,600 were in pickup trucks and vans, 4,600 on motorcycles, 800 in large trucks, and 900 on bicycles. Five hundred people died in railroad and subway accidents (although only five of them were passengers); 1,100 died in recreational boating accidents. (These ground statistics don't include accidents in pipelines, grade crossings, or commercial boats.)

In contrast, 900 people died in general aviation (private plane) accidents (a 10 percent decrease since 1984 and the lowest level in history), 77 in air taxies, 35

89

in commuter airlines, and 197 in the U.S. scheduled air carriers.

Lest these figures do the opposite of what they're intended to do and scare you off *all* forms of transportation, consider that passenger cars—the most dangerous form of transportation—killed only half as many people a year as alcoholic beverages and only a third as many as those 150,000 who die from smoking.

Before examining specific accidents, let's first consider ways in which press coverage influences our perceptions of safety. Nobody would deny that 1985 was an unfortunate one for the airline industry worldwide. In a year that saw history's largest single plane accident (in Japan), the explosion of a trans-Atlantic flight (Air India's), one bad U.S. crash (in Dallas), and three frightening hijackings, it's not surprising that flight safety was in the news. But the sheer mass of news coverage was bound to push the level of concern beyond what the facts allow.

Do Tom Brokaw (NBC) or Dan Rather (CBS) ever open their nightly news program with this kind of bulletin: "One hundred twenty-three people were killed today—some were mangled, some crushed, several were burned to death, and a few were decapitated"? No. You won't hear that because the same thing happened yesterday, it will happen again tomorrow, and the day after, and the day after that. One hundred twenty-three is the average number of people killed each day on our nation's highways.

No, you don't hear that kind of news. That more than 45,000 people lose their lives every year through highway fatalities (half caused by drunken drivers) is not news. It's predictable. It's constant. It's a way of life—or a way of death. It's not news.

But it is prime time news in all the media if one big Boeing 747 lands with one blown tire (they have seventeen others), or one engine malfunctions (the 747 flies very well on three engines, even on two). Or if any "authority" makes a public pronouncement stating that some controllers are overworked, or some engines are faulty, or some airports are unsafe, or some pilots are inadequately trained, or the skies are too crowded. Aviation accidents, or incidents, receive exaggerated coverage. The *Washington Post* gave the January 13, 1982, Air Florida crash front-page coverage, with pictures, for nine consecutive days.

The U.S. scheduled air carriers' safety record merits our attention. Here are some facts:

The U.S. scheduled air carriers are now transporting daily an average of one million people an average distance of close to 1,000 miles.

How safely have they been doing this? During the three years before the August 2, 1985, L-1011 crash at Dallas/Fort Worth, more than one billion people were carried through 15 million takeoffs and landings in all kinds of weather with a fatality toll of only forty-eight people.

The average annual fatality rate for the U.S. scheduled airlines over the past five years (including 1985) was ninety. The average annual fatality rate on our nation's highways during the same five-year period has been 45,000.

To establish an accurate comparison between highway and airway travel, two factors must be considered. Although 45,000 is the annual average highway rate, the yearly average death rate resulting from passenger travel in *private automobiles* is 24,000. So let's take a closer look at the relative safety of private automobiles and the U.S. scheduled airlines.

Intercity Passenger Travel in the United States
(Passenger Miles in Millions)

	1981	1982	1983	1984	1985
Auto-mobiles	1,344,000	1,369,500	1,393,000	1,465,000	1,484,200
Airlines	201,434	213,002	232,200	250,700	277,200

	Yearly Average	*Ratio*
Automobiles	1,411,000	6
Airliners	235,000	1

This chart shows the ratio of automobile passenger miles to air-carrier passenger miles. Note that the automobile miles are six times greater.

Passenger Fatalities in the U.S.

	1981	1982	1983	1984	1985
Automobiles	26,555	23,330	22,979	23,490	23,600
Airliners	4	233	15	4	197

	Yearly Average
Automobiles	24,000
Airliners	90

SUMMATION

In *Passenger Miles,* the comparative yearly average of auto and airline is six-to-one (1,411 trillion to 234 billion).

In *Travel Fatalities,* the comparative yearly average must allow for the six-to-one ratio of passenger miles. Therefore, the automobile figure can either be divided by six or the airline figure increased six times. Either way, the comparative statistical relationship is forty-four to one.

(The information used here was taken from the annual safety reports of the National Transportation Safety Board in Washington, D.C., and from annual reports of the Air Transport Association of America, Washington, D.C.)

Those of you who feel safer in a car than in a plane because in a car you're "in control" should ask yourselves: Are you really in control? Isn't your survival on the highway dependent on the competence and sobriety of the drivers in the cars passing you or coming toward you? Half of the daily 123 fatalities are attributed to drunk driving. Relinquishing control to the pilots up front may make you nervous, but I can assure you that they are competently and soberly driving an air machine as infallible as man has yet devised.

H. W. Lewis, a professor of physics at the University of California at Santa Barbara, made the following assessment in the *Los Angeles Times* on September 1, 1985:

In recent times the record of America's scheduled airlines has averaged out to about one fatality per billion passenger miles. For a frequent traveler who, for example, averages well over 100,000 miles per year in commercial airlines, this means a chance of getting killed of about one in 10,000 per year. That is not far from the average probability of being murdered, or, indeed, of committing suicide. . . . We tend to worry about the wrong things, if we want to reduce our risk of premature demise—and who doesn't? It is true that 500 people died in the Japanese tragedy—it was a record. Yet *each day* close to 150 people die, just as tragically, in automobile accidents in the United States alone, and each day nearly 1000 people die in the United States as a direct consequence of smoking. One searches in vain for commensurate media coverage, and our fears are conditioned by the media.

Now recall another example of press influence on our consciousness: in 1985, some 10,000 people died in a cyclone in Bangladesh, compared with a world total of some 2,000 in commercial aircraft. Do you remember a magazine cover depicting those cyclone victims? Probably not, but surely you remember a number of covers with burnt-out fuselages on them. The media go for the spectacular.

Now newspapers are usually correct, but when it comes to aviation accidents or incidents, they are unbelievably incorrect and assumptive. I recently read a newspaper account of an airplane that stopped on the runway because of a fire in one of its engines. An engine fire can easily be put out by the systems on board the airplane itself, but because this one stopped before taking off, the local fire department came out to assist the operation. One of the firefighters was quoted as saying that if the plane had taken off, it certainly would have crashed. Now, I'm sorry, but that fireman had no knowledge of what would happen if an airplane took off with a fire. The truth of the matter is that taking off with a fire in the engine is not dangerous. Extinguishing a fire in flight is a standard procedure drilled into all airline pilots. Although it very seldom happens, it's not a perilous situation.

I mention this not to criticize the media, but to make you aware of how disproportionately you are affected by it. If you would like to be able to fly comfortably, I suggest you start collecting the *good* news about the safety of airline travel. Prejudiced people hear only what fits their prejudices, and you are prejudiced— admit it. Your past judgment has been based on feelings rather than facts.

"Yes, but what about crashes that *have* occurred?" The accounts that follow are for U.S. scheduled airlines, which account for 95 percent of all intercity air travel in the U.S. Commuter service, air taxis, and charters are not included. The civilian airliner carrying American soldiers that crashed in Gander, Newfoundland, in December 1985 was a charter flight. As a matter of interest, before this accident there had been no crashes of charters in 1984, nor in five of the past ten years.

Accidents on foreign airlines also have not been included, so there will be no account of the 1985 Air India and Japan Airlines accidents, for example. Suffice to say that most major foreign airlines adhere to safety standards that are similar to those in the U.S. Your chances of being in an accident on one of the major foreign airliners are still absurdly low.

The following material was compiled from several sources, most notably from data supplied by the National Transportation Safety Board. These accounts are for all accidents on the U.S. scheduled airlines over the five-year period between 1981 and 1985.

- There were no fatal crashes in 1981. There were four separate freak accidents that resulted in the only four fatalities recorded for U.S. scheduled carriers in that year. Two of these fatalities involved ground personnel, one was a flight attendant who was killed in a galley elevator, and one was a passenger who fell off a boarding ladder.

- Three air crashes accounted for all fatalities on scheduled carriers in 1982. The first was a World Airways flight that went off the runway at Logan International on January 23. At first no casualties were reported, since the plane had come to a halt in a few feet of water with no major damage to its structure. Later it was discovered that two people had disappeared, probably during the evacuation, and were presumed drowned.

- On January 13, an Air Florida Boeing 737 crashed shortly after taking off from Washington National Airport. The existing ice and snow conditions called for the use of anti-icing. One airline-pilot witness said that the plane was covered with ice and snow "from the nose to the tail." The National Transportation Board investigators discovered, however, that the cockpit voice recorder indicated a reply of "off" to the standard checklist query, "anti-ice?" The cockpit anti-ice switches were recovered in the "off" position. Ice accumulating on the wing and tail surfaces would have seriously impaired lifting or flight characteristics and resulted in a stall condition. Seconds after takeoff, and until impact with the bridge, the distinct noise of the stall-warning device could be heard on the recording tape. Icing, incidentally, was a big problem with propeller airplanes. It is not considered a problem with jets. The powerful jet engines provide ample hot air to de-ice the flight surfaces, the engine cowlings, and their accessories.

A number of people suggested at the time that National Airport itself was unsafe. It is unfair to blame the airport for that tragedy. B-737s of equivalent weight regularly lift off that runway using just 3,700 of the 6,879 available feet. Three hundred and fifty thousand flights land and take off at National yearly, with the annual passenger limit now set at 16 million. There hadn't been a crash at that airport since 1949.

The Washington crash occurred after twenty-six months without a single fatal accident on U.S. scheduled airlines. This record was set in 1980 and 1981 during a period when, in a statement made by the Federal Aviation Administration, "Airlines flew more than a half-billion passengers on more than 10 million flights." That works out to more than a half-trillion passenger miles—enough to take every man, woman, and child in America on a flight of more than 2,000 miles.

• On July 9, a Pan Am 727 crashed into a residential area shortly after takeoff from New Orleans Moissant Airport, killing all 145 passengers and crew aboard. Severe thunderstorms were recorded in the immediate vicinity at the time of takeoff, and wind shear was listed as the likely primary cause. (See discussion section at the end of this chapter for more on this type of windshear.)

- There were four accidents in 1983, which claimed fifteen lives. An Air Illinois flight taking off from Pinkneyville, Illinois, crashed on takeoff, killing all ten people aboard. The pilot flew into a thunderstorm, which resulted in an electrical failure on board. At this point the pilot could have easily returned to Pinkneyville and landed safely. Instead, he chose to fly on emergency battery power to a distant airport, and crashed when this second power supply gave out. This is considered a highly unusual, almost freakish set of circumstances.

- The other fatalities in 1983 included a man operating a snow sweeper who was killed when he was struck by the wing of a landing plane, three crewmembers who died in the crash of a cargo flight, and one passenger who was killed when a piece of the wing broke into the cabin when a plane hit a snowbank while landing.

- 1984 saw a single fatal accident when three crewmembers and one nonpaying passenger were killed in a cargo flight.

- On January 1, 1985, an Eastern Airlines Boeing 727 bound for a landing in La Paz, Bolivia, flew into a mountain during descent from cruise altitude. The cause of the crash is still unknown because the flight recorder could not be recovered from the deep snow in the mountain. This was the first catastrophe involving a major U.S. airline in thirty months.

- On May 31, a cargo plane operated by General Aviation, Inc., crashed during final approach to Nashville when it flew through a windshear. The two crewmembers lost their lives.

- On August 2, a Delta L-1011 crashed while attempting to land at Dallas/Fort Worth International Airport. One hundred sixty-three passengers were killed; twenty-nine survived. Preliminary reports conclude that a microburst, a rare form of windshear caused by a strong downward blast of wind that occurs very infrequently beneath some rain clouds, was the cause. (See section on windshear in the discussion section at the end of this chapter.)

- The last fatal accident on a U.S. scheduled carrier in 1985 was the August 6 crash of a Midwest Express DC-9 shortly after takeoff, when one engine failed and the second lost power. Thirty-one passengers and crew were killed. Causes are still under investigation.

Those of you who have not flown enough to work through your fear will defend yourselves by citing recent disasters and shaking your heads. The rest of you will express concern about those tragedies, but you will go on about the business and pleasure of living and flying, recognizing that it is still far safer to fly than to drive and that a million people in the U.S. do it every day without incident or accident.

The next time you find yourself ogling over some tabloid description of a tire blowout on a 747, run the following sentences through your head: "I'm afraid to get in my car and drive anywhere because 123 people are going to be killed in cars today in America, and I could be one of them. After all, I have been lucky for the last (ten, twenty, thirty, forty, etc.) years—my number must be about up!" Those thoughts don't keep you from driving, do they?

As far as the air tragedies of 1985 go, consider the following passage from *Time* on January 13, 1986:

Despite the unusual number of mishaps in 1985, air travel remains comparatively safe. The chances of perishing in an air accident last year were 1 in 600,000. That was up sharply from 1 to 3.7 million in 1984, but still compares favorably with other forms of travel. On a mile-for-mile basis, Americans are nearly 100 times as likely to die in car accidents as in plane crashes. Secor Browne, former chairman of the Civil Aeronautics Board and now a Washington consultant, calls aviation easily "the safest mode of transportation." He adds, "If you're afraid to fly, then you'd better not take a bath, and God forbid, don't get in your car."

The spate of 1985 air accidents seems to have affected the travel plans of very few flyers. A CBS poll in August 1985, which asked flyers if they had canceled or changed plans to fly after the Dallas and Japan crashes, revealed that only 5 percent of the flyers had done so—leaving 95 percent who didn't.

If the safety figures don't do it for you, it might help you to consider what an ordinary occurrence flying is in today's world. Some thirty years ago, only about 10 percent of the U.S. population had traveled on an airliner. An October 1979 Gallup survey for the Air Transportation Association of America showed that 65 percent of the adult population in the United States had flown on a commercial airliner—120 million people. In 1984, according to the Air Transport Association, the airlines accounted for more than 88 percent of the miles of intercity public passenger traffic in the U.S., up from 80 percent ten years previously. Between cities, the airlines carry six times more people than buses and trains carry.

As helpful and as important as these facts are, they will not make the truly fearful flyer less afraid. As I have already said, if your fears were rational, then a rational discussion of the risks involved would eliminate your fears. The mere fact that an average of 7,000 pedestrians die in accidents every year from *walking* ought to alter your feelings about flying at least slightly.

The rest of this chapter will be devoted to a question-and-answer session on the general subject of flying today. The questions are based on those that seminar participants have asked over the years, and they run the gamut from the air controllers' strike to windshear. In the course of allaying your fears, the answers to these questions will also provide some interesting reading. Read through them someday on a long flight!

DISCUSSION

I read a lot about how the airlines are pinched for funds since deregulation and that they are cutting back on employees and on service. Isn't there a tendency to cut back on maintenance also?

The one area that is immune from cutbacks is the quality and quantity of engine and aircraft maintenance. Safety is the primary concern of the industry and its government agencies, and there are no compromises. The F.A.A. (Federal Aviation Administration), the insurance companies, the airlines, and the pilots and mechanics are all in agreement on this. Planes are monitored by hand, eye, and electronics on the ground and in flight. The monitoring and maintenance cycle begins while the plane is being built and continues through the life of its service. A plane will be grounded if a piece of its equipment is a few thousandths of an inch out of position, even though the problem would have to be many times greater to cause any serious trouble.

Despite unsettling media stories about so-called overworked controllers, unsafe airports, and poorly trained flight crews, our skies are distinctly safer than ever before. Safer, even though during the past ten years there has been a 70 percent increase in the number of passengers carried compared to the previous ten years. Additionally, the accident rate from 1976 through 1985 has been *less than half* of what it was from 1966 through 1975.

How old are most airline pilots and how much training are they really given?

The Airline Pilots Association, which represents 39,000 pilots in all but one of the major U.S. scheduled airlines and between twenty and thirty commuter airlines, notes that the average age of its member pilots is forty-five, and that their average length of service with their current airlines is seventeen years.

Pilots enter the major carriers either after thorough training as military pilots or by starting out in small, private planes-for-hire services and working their way slowly up through air taxi services, small commuter airlines, and larger commuter airlines before they have the basic credentials to apply to the major airlines after 2,000 to 3,000 hours of flight experience. All major U.S. carriers operate on a seniority system for pilots, and even seasoned professionals start at the "bottom" in the cockpit, as a flight engineer—not even flying—on a 727 or DC-10, or as a copilot on a two-pilot plane like a 737. From there, it will take another five or ten years just to become a copilot or pilot. The average *junior* pilot at United Airlines, for example, has seventeen years of experience with that airline.

Airline hiring procedures are even more rigorous than the prerequisite qualifying experience. Pilot applicants are subjected to a battery of physical, psychological, and aptitude tests. They also submit to a peer review by managing pilots or line pilots, who check not only for a thorough knowledge of flying and skill but also for the applicant's ability to get along with others in the cockpit. In the end, the number of applicants can be anywhere from five to fifteen times higher than the number accepted.

After they are hired, pilots go through extensive training regardless of their qualifications, including six to eight weeks of ground training, classroom work, simulations, and test flights.

The training never stops. Throughout their careers, pilots are constantly subjected to tests, including an annual in-flight inspection by the company and/or an FAA official, and if either notes problems with technique or textbook knowledge, the pilot can be sent back for retraining. Every six months, the pilot must take refresher courses, during which flight knowledge and proficiency are once again reviewed.

In addition, all pilots are given routine refresher training and training for modifications and improvement in their aircraft totaling a month each year. It takes about two months of ground and flight training for an airline pilot to upgrade to another type of aircraft. To get all checked out or "rated," as it is called, the pilot must pass several written, oral, and flight examinations that deal with every conceivable abnormality or emergency.

Pilots are also given intensive medical checkups twice each year by F.A.A.-approved doctors. Medical conditions that would result in a mild prescription and advice to take a day's rest often ground a pilot for weeks or months. Sixty is the mandatory retirement age for pilots on major commercial carriers.

How much time does the average pilot spend on the job of flying, and how much do pilots get paid?

A four-year study completed in 1980 by the Civil Aeronautics Board showed that the cockpit crewmembers of nine major airlines averaged 556 productive hours yearly. ("Productive" was considered to be the time between departure from the gate for a flight and return to the gate.) With allowance for a month's vacation, that figures out to an average of forty-seven flight hours a month. The average salary for an A.L.P.A. pilot is $80,000 a year. A 747 captain commanding international flights receives considerably more than that.

How many pilots are there up front, and is the number changing with new planes?

All four- and three-engine jets use three pilots. The third cockpit crewmember serves as flight engineer but is also trained as a pilot. The twin-engine transports are usually flown by two pilots. This includes most Boeing 757s and 767s. The Airline Pilots Association fought hard for the three-pilot crew concept but finally agreed to accept the decision of an appointed presidential task force for two. The task force concluded that "a third pilot would not be justified in the interest of safety." A strong consideration must have been that the safety record for jets crewed by two pilots has been as good, even a little better, than those crewed by three. The wide-bodied, long-range jets will continue to use a crew of three.

Have any of the airlines hired women pilots?

A few have. There are about 400 women in the A.L.P.A. today. The reason there aren't more female airline pilots is that in the recent past the airlines had their pick of well-qualified, experienced, male, military jet pilots who had left the service to join the airlines.

A pilot who lives down the street from me was taken off flying status for several months because of an automobile accident. I understand that he had to go back to school before he could resume flying. Is this true?

All airline pilots are given training and competency checks every six months. This includes a ground school assignment and a flight proficiency check. Their skills at handling normal, abnormal, and emergency flight conditions are reviewed. To remain "legal" on the aircraft for which he has qualified, your neighbor must make a minimum of three takeoffs and landings every ninety days.

Company check pilots and Federal Aviation Administration flight inspectors often ride in the cockpit to observe, and make note of, the pilots' proficiency, procedures, judgment, etc. No other profession is as closely monitored.

Before your friend was approved for a return to flight status, he probably had to take a complete physical examination. Two a year are a government requirement. The airline companies require an additional examination by their own medical staff.

I read about a captain on one of the big jets who suffered a fatal heart attack about an hour before landing in San Francisco. The copilot made the landing without a problem, but what if that captain had had his heart attack as he was making the takeoff?

The airplane is equipped with dual flight controls and duplicate flight instrumentation. Both pilots are equally qualified to fly the airplane. While one is landing, or taking off, the other is closely monitoring the procedure and could immediately take over if the need arose. You don't have that backup protection in your automobile, but you most assuredly have it on an airliner.

What about the flight service attendants' training?

The airlines are very selective in the hiring of flight attendants. Education, health, work experience, communication skills, and an ability to deal pleasantly and effectively with all kinds of people are some of the minimum requirements.

The initial training is usually accomplished over an intensive five-week period. Since passenger safety is the flight attendants' primary responsibility, special attention is given to familiarization with all emergency and safety features of the aircraft. This includes evacuation on land and at sea. (Before the F.A.A. allows any U.S.

commercial jet to carry passengers, the airline and the manufacturer must demonstrate that a full load of passengers—about 400 in the case of a 747—can be evacuated completely in only ninety seconds with half the plane's exits blocked.) First aid and CPR are also taught. Near the completion of their training, all attendants must complete in-flight training under supervision.

Recurrent testing and training are conducted twice a year. Flight attendants must take requalification training if they have not taken training for twelve months.

There still must be a shortage of trained air traffic controllers. Didn't that strike seriously endanger our air transport system?

No. It didn't. On August 31, 1981, when 13,000 members of the Professional Air Traffic Controllers Organization (P.A.T.C.O.) failed to report for work, it looked as if they had almost immobilized the industry. But those who came back, or who had stayed on, plus supervisors and military controllers, kept the system operating by cutting operations back to a safe and reasonable level.

Spokesmen for P.A.T.C.O. implied that the skies were unsafe, that their services were indispensable. Their propaganda started to wear thin when the public realized that their demands were out of line and that the system could function without them because the government had prepared for such a contingency.

Within a few days, my pilot friends began telling me that the system was working safely and smoothly. Today our traffic control network is functioning as well as ever.

FREEDOM FROM FEAR OF FLYING

One of my biggest worries is what would happen if I were up there about seven miles and one of the engines caught fire.

Good question! First, all engines—steam, piston, or jet—use fire to generate the combustion-expansion cycle that provides power. Of the three power sources, the jet engine is the simplest and the safest. And it's simple to handle in case of fire.

There are several strategically located fire detector sensors around those engines. When an overheating condition is detected, an alarm goes off in the cockpit, and a flashing red light indicates which engine has the problem. The "fire drill" is thorough and routine. A lever (actually it is called a "T" handle) is pulled, which isolates the affected engine from all fuel, oil, hydraulic, and electrical sources. This should eliminate the fire. However, if an indication of fire still exists, a powerful extinguisher can be directed to the area. A spare supply is also available.

I sometimes like to shock people by telling them that I had to deal with more than 200 engine fires during my career as a Pan Am pilot. But I'm quick to add that they all occurred during the realistic and thorough simulator training that all pilots are regularly required to complete. I certainly was well trained to handle a difficulty that, in thirty-one years, never happened. Now, as a passenger, I can easily doze off in the cabin because I know how safe the plane is and how carefully selected and highly trained the crews are.

When you are up there in the clouds, how do you avoid colliding with other planes?

We have several backup systems. Flying in the clouds is strictly prohibited except by qualified pilots who have filed an instrument flight plan and have been assigned a flight altitude and routing by an air traffic control center. Roughly, eastbound flights fly at odd altitudes of 27,000, 29,000, or 31,000 feet, etc. Westbound flights fly at even altitudes. So the height separation is 1,000 feet. Laterally, the separation is ten miles. Our navigational and autopilot accommodations guide us right down the middle, giving us a five-mile margin on either side. Overland flights are also closely monitored by the ever-surveillant radar stations. Long, overwater flights are separated 2,000 feet vertically and fifty miles laterally.

I get very nervous when we start circling in the clouds before landing. Isn't there a danger of collision?

No. That "circling" is actually a holding pattern, precisely flown in a racetracklike shape in designated areas within a few minutes' access of the airport. The planes are "stacked up" with a vertical separation of 1,000 feet and the plane's position is closely monitored on radar. When the plane at the bottom of the stack is cleared to approach and land, the others are individually, and sequentially, instructed to descend to an assigned altitude 1,000 feet below their previous altitude.

On a recent flight from Los Angeles to Chicago, we must have circled for almost an hour before we descended and landed. I was concerned that we might be getting low on fuel.

Whether you were being held up because of traffic, weather, or both, fuel was not a problem. To meet F.A.A. fuel requirements, your aircraft was provided with sufficient fuel to fly from Los Angeles to Chicago, then make an approach to land, then to pull up and proceed to any one of a half-dozen suitable airports and still hold for thirty minutes before descending to land. Remember, that's the minimum! A little information from the cockpit could have put you at ease.

I'm scared of thunderstorms and lightning. We flew through a storm recently, and I have never been so frightened in my life!

You felt fear, so you concluded that the occurrence was dangerous. I want to point out, again, that your fears about flight experiences are not derived from facts—only from feelings. We generally avoid thunderstorms. We fly over them or around them. If we choose to fly through a mild one, we will slow the aircraft down as you would with your car when you encounter a rough road. Our aircraft radar, and that used by the air traffic controllers on the ground, can easily determine the size and intensity of storms. The controllers are skilled professionals, and they can clear us to another altitude or routing more comfortable for the passengers. Flying through storms may be uncomfortable, but it is not unsafe.

Lightning is a spectacular and awesome sight, and —in your case—also terrifying. However, you were not imperiled. An aircraft is a completed bonded metal conductor, and a lightning strike would not penetrate into the interior or disable the aircraft. Lightning injures and kills hundreds of people yearly on the ground, but you are always safe from lightning in a plane, even when the plane is on the ground.

Turbulence really scares me. When that plane starts shaking, I start shaking, too.

As to the airplane shaking, as long as your seat belt is fastened, turbulence will not hurt you. Nor is it a threat to the structure of the aircraft, which is as rugged and strong as a battleship. Most of the time, for passenger comfort, rough weather is avoided by flying over or around it.

Flying through turbulent air can be compared to the jolt of riding a speedboat on a choppy lake or the bounce of driving your car over a potholed city street or a chuck-holed country road.

As for your shaking, it is an involuntary response to your nervousness. Speed up the shaking. That will put you back in control. Then, being in control, you can gradually stop it. Also, practice turbulent flying at home. Bounce up and down in your chair. Suppose you are on an airliner and there has been an indication that there will be turbulence. In anticipation, bounce up and down with your seat belt fastened comfortably. Someone always says, "I will feel silly practicing for turbulence." Well, isn't feeling silly better than feeling scared?

Besides thunderstorms, what else can cause turbulence?

"Turbulence" is an alarming word and often used over the public address system to describe any air that is not perfectly smooth. Choppiness is what is usually encountered in unstable air. Air is always in motion. Even in a quiet room smoke from a cigarette can be observed to waft and curl. Air in rapid motion becomes wind. A steady wind becomes gusty and unsteady when it moves across uneven terrain in the same way that water becomes choppy when it moves over a shallow, rocky riverbed.

Clear Air Turbulence (CAT), occurs at flight altitudes when two air streams, traveling at different speeds, converge. The air is disturbed and choppy where they meet and blend. Imagine two fast-moving streams coming together to move on as a river. That surface will also be choppy. CAT is rare, and won't interfere with the normal functioning of the airplane. In *Frequent Flyer* magazine, Patrick Clyne, a Northwest Orient pilot and coordinator of the A.L.P.A.'s severe-weather-data projects, said, "Probably 99.99 percent of the flights never encounter it." It is usually of short duration.

But because CAT has caused a very few passenger injuries, the industry is examining ways to pinpoint it, including a device that could detect the conditions for CAT from 100 miles away.

Just to put *all* types of turbulence into perspective, compare the bumpiest plane ride you can remember to *any* bus ride, cab ride, or train ride you can recall. Air turbulence rarely gets as bad as normal surface public transportation.

What about windshear?

Windshear may be dreaded by the fearful flyer, but it has been with us since the Wright brothers. Windshear occurs in an area where two air masses, moving at different speeds and direction, converge. The reaction in this shear area could be compared to the disturbed surface of water that results if two streams, one slow and one fast, intersect. Windshear can occur in the vicinity of thunderstorms and is, in fact, occasionally encountered in flight as simple choppiness.

It is a hazard to airliners only at low levels of flight

during the approach to landing or on takeoff. Windshear has caused three airline crashes in the past twelve years. The first one was at New York's Kennedy Airport, the second at New Orleans in 1982, and the last, in August 1985, at the Dallas–Fort Worth Airport.

Transportation Secretary Elizabeth Dole announced in April 1986 that the government would soon be ready to install at major airports advanced radar equipment capable of detecting windshear. Meanwhile 110 airports have been equipped with the best equipment now available.

Airline manufacturers are now building on-board windshear detection and avoidance systems into new model jetliners, including the new Airbus A320 and the Boeing 737-300.

The best prevention besides detection is training pilots to handle such situations correctly, and the government is currently spending $1.7 million to train pilots to avoid the sudden wind shifts with the help of digital simulators that provide windshear flight experience.

I hope that it is some consolation to you that your odds of being on a flight imperiled by windshear are 20 million to one—and improving.

I wonder about the movement of the wings. Sometimes they seem to flap like a bird's.

Indeed they do, in choppy and uneven air. Wings are not rigid; their strength is in their flexibility. They are designed and extensively tested to flex eight feet up or down at the wing tip. In 1982 Boeing, in a ground test, pushed the wings of a 767 to fifteen feet without negative effects. Jet aircraft wings are built to withstand the most rugged storms, just as a battleship can withstand the most turbulent seas. But a jet can avoid storms, and a battleship cannot.

I just had a real scare. It was snowing and windy at the Indianapolis Airport, and the first time we came in to land, the plane suddenly pulled up. Within a few minutes the same thing happened again. I was sick with fear. No announcement was made. Several people looked terrified. We landed on the third try. I was so scared I couldn't move. Two people came and helped me off the plane. I haven't flown since.

I doubt you were exposed to any danger. Most of your fright was caused by not knowing what was going on and feeling helpless. The gross error was the lack of any explanation from the cockpit. Flight crews are all too often guilty of failing to use the public address system when, to the passenger, it may well make the difference between being mildly uncomfortable and being a "nervous wreck." The first responsibility of the pilot is safety; the second is concern for the passengers' comfort. In this case, the latter was ignored. As a pilot, I know there was time for a brief explanation over the P.A.

Passengers who are treated so insensitively should write a letter to the president of the offending airline, giving the flight number, date, and circumstances. They might also send a copy to the Federal Aviation Administration in Washington, D.C., and to the Airline Passengers Association in Dallas.

What would happen if a tire blew out?

If you are speaking of the front tire on your automobile, you have a dangerous problem. But there are multiple tires on airliners, and if one were to blow, it would make little or no difference. Aircraft tires are much more reliable than automobile tires. In thirty-one years of airline flying, I can recall having two blowouts, and neither was a problem. The 747 distributes its weight over *eighteen* tires.

What about hijacking and terrorism?

A 1985 poll conducted for CBS "Morning News" confirmed what most of us have become aware of: the threat of terrorism is almost twice as alarming to the general public as the fear of accidents.

Incidents of violence and hijacking have a tremendous impact on our thoughts as television presents them in vivid detail. In an article in *U.S. News and World Report,* Professor Neil Postman of New York University comments, ". . . images exacerbate people's sense of how significant these events are in the world scene. The cumulative effect of seeing an airliner 1,000 times with a hole in it almost makes it seem as if it has happened 1,000 times. . . . One has the sense that without television month after month showing Qaddafi's face and terrorism's carnage, Libya's presence would have been largely ignored."

Be assured that preventing these incidents has become the top concern of the airline industry. Better detection of weapons at airports further reduces the chances of terror in the air. Improved X-ray equipment and mechanical sniffers are already in use at a number of U.S. airports, and the F.A.A. is funding several research projects to develop new ways to detect bombs.

The risk of terrorism, like the fear of flying, must be assessed realistically rather than emotionally. Be aware that U.S. airlines carry almost 400 million people every year. This should help you recognize that a given individual's odds of being involved in any violent incident are very small indeed. In fact, the number of Americans killed in *all* terrorist incidents (in aircraft or otherwise) in 1984 and 1985 was forty-one, lower than ten years previously and exponentially lower than the *17,000* people murdered in the U.S. in 1984.

I think that some of the runways used by these big jets are simply not long enough.

All jet transports, 747s included, use less than two-thirds of the runway for takeoff (usually about one-half). Runways of even minimum length are required to have ample distance for the pilot to accelerate up to takeoff speed and then, if a problem occurs, abort the takeoff and brake to a stop within two-thirds of the length of the runway. Additional distance is required if the runway is wet. The required length of the runway for takeoff or landing depends upon the type of aircraft, weight, temperature, and prevailing wind conditions. When your pilot lands and doesn't turn off until near the end of the runway, he adds to your comfort by little or no braking. With maximum braking, he could probably turn off less than halfway down the runway.

I watched one of the big jets coming in to land the other day. It seemed dangerously slow to me. Wasn't it very close to stalling?

No. The speed maintained at all phases of the landing approach is at least 30 percent above the stall speed, based on a consideration of weight and the degrees of flap setting. Jumbo jets appear to fly slowly because of their immense size. A small executive jet at the same speed seems to streak through the air twice as fast.

Why do planes fly so high?

Height gives us several advantages. The air at 30,000 feet is less than half as dense as the air at 5,000 feet. Thinner air offers less resistance and allows us to fly at more than twice the speed available at the lower altitude. We use less fuel up there, too, because fuel consumption decreases in proportion to the decrease in air density. Besides, it's smoother high above the clouds.

In an accident investigation, I once heard a reporter refer to a "black box." What is it? What does it do?

The so-called black box is actually orange. It is a flight data recorder and is located in the tail section of all U.S. air carriers. This almost indestructible electronic device records the time, speed, altitude, and direction of the aircraft. All movement is recorded: climbing, descending, turning, gravitational forces, and acceleration. The recorder contains information vital to any accident investigation. So does the cockpit voice recorder, a microphone in the ceiling of the cockpit of every jetliner that records all the sounds, noises, and conversations that take place in the cockpit. It, too, must be on during all phases of flight and ground operations.

I recently saw what appeared to be smoke coming out of the side vents in the cabin. I thought it might be an electrical fire. The flight attendant told me that it was nothing to worry about, but what caused it?

If you were to go to your refrigerator on a warm, humid day and open the freezer door, the same thing would happen. When cold air hits warm moist air, condensation, or vapor, is formed. The same thing can happen when the aircraft air conditioning is turned on. Sometimes even drops of water may fall from an overhead vent. It's moisture, not a leaky roof.

Why do some planes start to shake during the descent?

During the descent in an aircraft such as the Boeing 727, "speed brakes" are commonly used to reduce speed. These brakes are more appropriately called "spoilers" because they "spoil" the smooth air flow over the wing. Some pilots will use them more than others. The next time you feel the plane "trembling" during the descent, look out at the top of the wing, and you may see these spoilers raised at an angle of between ten and thirty degrees.

Note how smooth the ride becomes when they are retracted. Landing flaps will also create some vibration, but they are quite different in that they extend back and down from the trailing edge of the wing. They slow the aircraft during the approach and the landing. After landing, the spoilers are raised to an almost vertical position to aid in braking. They are easy to see if you are sitting over the wing.

If my car engine conks out, I can always pull over and call for help. But if a plane engine went, wouldn't it be all over?

No. All jet transports are multi-engined, and each engine is much more reliable than your auto engine. A four-engine jet flies safely on three or two engines, and a three or two-engine jet can fly safely on one. A 747 at 35,000 feet, with all engines *off*, can glide for 150 miles. The air has substance and will carry an aerodynamically sound object for quite a while.

All right. Let's just cover the worst-case scenario. What if I'm in a plane crash?

According to an article in the April 1985 issue of *Frequent Flyer* magazine, "Roughly 80 percent of all plane crashes are survivable." The article went on to say that 40 percent of postcrash fatalities are fire-related and that the F.A.A. had followed through on many initiatives proposed by the agency in 1983 to reduce fire hazards. These include mandatory fire-resistant seat covers and other fire-blocking materials on all commercial airliners carrying thirty passengers or more.

I am disturbed by the strange sounds and movements in a plane.

Sudden movement in a car is accepted, while any movement in a plane is interpreted as ominous. You are likely to be unfamiliar, unaware, and uninformed about all the sounds, grunts, groans, lurchings, and squeaks of the modern-day jet. During a recent flight, a fearful flyer nervously asked me to identify so many sounds that even I, a forty-five-year veteran airman, was occasionally stumped. Identification of the sounds—the landing gear, flaps, and power supply—might be helpful, but all sounds, like all movements, must be *accepted* if one is to become comfortable. Explanations often elicit more questions. *Once you have learned to relax on board, your constant quest for ominous sounds*

119

will fade. Until you relax, expert answers won't help much.

It seems appropriate to end this chapter with a few thoughts about risk. From birth, which itself might be regarded as risky, people are taking risks as they reach out and explore. When we begin to walk, we risk falling. When we learn to ride a bicycle, we most certainly risk falling. All growth and learning involves risk. We take chances in everything we do.

The phobic person tries to avoid risk in a particular circumstance. Agoraphobics avoid anything unfamiliar and eventually retreat to the seeming security of the home, maybe even to one room in that home. But we who have a desire to live fully must risk adventures. We must also risk failure and embarrassment. It's simply the way a real life is lived. A man named John A. Shedd once wrote, "A sailing ship is safe in the harbor, but that's not where a sailing ship is meant to be."

In truth, flying is not risky in any objective sense of the word. The risks you encounter in flying are the risks of change in yourself. You risk being excited, being adventurous, confronting your fear; you risk growth.

Think of the risks you have taken until now, many of them far more dangerous than flying. Almost all of us have run a race, or patted a dog, or learned to swim, or ridden a horse. Most of us have leaned out of a second-story window, stood on a rooftop, sailed in a boat, walked alone at night, slept in a tent, stood outside and watched lightning, driven or walked through a rainstorm, swam across a stream, traveled to a new city, spoken to a stranger, ducked our heads underwater, or braved the excitement and agony of a first date, a first kiss.

Is there such a thing as total security? Has there ever been? Some fearful flyers seem to want an absolute guarantee of safety. No such thing exists or ever has. Life itself is tenuous, temporary, fragile. Who can even assure you that you will live out this day? The only certainty in life is its uncertainty, its unpredictability. Some find that threatening; some find it exciting.

The fearful flyer speaks of concern about safety but is actually threatened by his or her unpredictable response, the threat of emotions: "What will happen to *me?*" Flying will give you confidence in yourself, and confidence will inevitably lead to joy in life's unpredictability. Wouldn't it be a bore otherwise? As Helen Keller said, "Life is either an adventure or it is nothing."

CHAPTER V

THE PROCESS
OF FLIGHT

THE SMALL CESSNA 150S AND THE HUGE BOEING 747S USE
the same principles to become airborne: lift, power,
and direction.

Lift is the primary force of flight. Most of us have had
the childhood experience of putting our hand out of the
window of a rapidly moving car. As we tilted the palm
of our hand up, the air stream forced our hand upward,
and down if the palm was tilted downward. Most of us
discovered as children that kites climb into the skies if
there is a wind to lift them or that we could generate
our own lift without wind by running to get the kite up.
Olympic ski jumpers lean forward in midair for lift, as
well as balance.

Air provides lift for kites, gliders, birds, little 150s,
and big 747s. Air has density, weight, and substance.

Air does not have "pockets" or holes in it. The accompanying cross-section diagram of an airplane wing is slightly exaggerated to illustrate how the underside of the wing is flat compared to the camber, or curve, on the topside. Most of our lift comes from the topside. The air hitting the underside of the wing creates an upward *pushing* force. The air passing over the top of the wing creates an upward *lifting* force because the curve of the wing's topside causes the air to move faster, reducing its density and pressure. The wings (and the plane with it) respond to these pushing and lifting forces to create flight. In order to take advantage of this principle, a 747 (weighing up to 750,000 pounds) accelerates down the runway until it reaches a speed of about 180 mph. The pilot then lightly eases the control column back, the nose of the aircraft rises, and air passing under and over the wings creates lift-off.

Power: The jet engine became the power source for airline transports almost thirty years ago. That change from propellers to jets revolutionized the industry. The jet engine provides smoother, safer, less expensive, more reliable, and immensely more powerful transportation. It greatly expanded and improved the operational capabilities of airplanes, which consequently improved the professional standards of the people in the cockpit.

The jet engine is also a much simpler power source than the piston-propeller engine. It has fewer moving parts and is easier to maintain. The accompanying diagram may help to explain. Outside air is sucked into the front of the engine and compressed by a series of spinning, fanlike blades. This hot, compressed air is then mixed with fuel (which closely resembles kero-

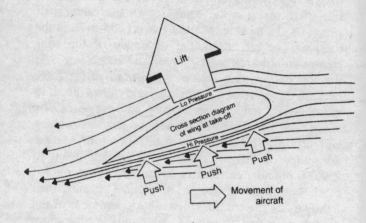

sene) and burned. The now hot, expanding air exits through the rear of the engine much faster than when it entered. On its way out, this exhaust passes through a turbine wheel attached to the same rotating shaft as the blades that first compressed it. The process of compression and combustion is thus continuous and self-sustaining. The plane, driven forward by its own exhaust, illustrates one of Sir Isaac Newton's laws of motion: for every action there is an equal and opposite reaction.

Direction: Both airplanes and boats use rudders for directional control. In a boat, the rudder is a movable, vertical control located in the aft section in the fluid called water. An airplane rudder is located in the tail

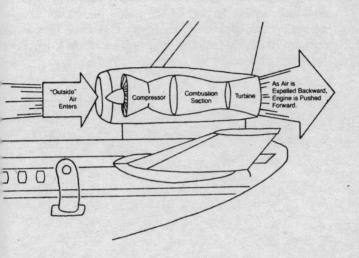

section and makes a similar vertical movement in the fluid called air. (Physicists designate both air and water as fluids.) Turns in an airplane are smoothly coordinated with the use of ailerons, movable flight surfaces located in the rear edges of the wings. Climbing and descending are directed by moving the horizontal tail surfaces called elevators. The actions of turning, climbing, and descending are initiated by the pilot at the flight controls. Otherwise aircraft will fly straight and level: they do not fall or tip over.

The transport jets, which fly faster and more economically at high altitudes, all cruise at about 550 miles per hour at an altitude of 35,000 feet.

125

Another measure of speed is expressed in terms of Mach: the speed of sound. 550 miles per hour is close to .80 Mach, or 80 percent of the speed of sound. The British-French supersonic transport *Concorde* flies at altitudes of 60,000 feet and at speeds of Mach 2, twice the speed of sound.

CHAPTER VI

AN OCEAN CROSSING

This chapter aims to put the information about flying in previous chapters into its everyday context by giving you a behind-the-scenes look at a typical scheduled flight aboard a large jet transport. This description will cover everything from preflight inspections, to in-flight navigation, to taxiing after landing, so that you can see how the entire process of a scheduled flight is accomplished.

For this imaginary journey, I've chosen the ocean crossing between New York's Kennedy Airport and London's Heathrow Airport. I will be your pilot. I made this trip hundreds of times in my career as the pilot of a Boeing 707, but to keep current with the constantly advancing technology of airliners, I'll describe this crossing as it occurs today in a Boeing 747.

Most of these flights depart in the early evening, say seven P.M., and arrive in London about seven A.M. the following morning. London time is five hours earlier than New York's so unless you advance your watch, you'll be reading two A.M. on arrival in London.

The flight crew's job begins when we—the captain, copilot (often called first officer), and flight engineer—arrive at the operations office an hour and a half before scheduled departure. The next twenty to thirty minutes are spent checking the computerized flight plan that has been prepared by the flight operations staff. The flight dispatcher will join us in reviewing the weather locally, en route, at our destination, and at alternate airports. Our takeoff weight, cruising altitude, estimated flight time, and weather conditions at destination all figure in the computation of the amount of fuel required. Included also is ample fuel to fly to any of several alternate airports (Shannon, Ireland; Prestwick, Scotland; Paris or Amsterdam) in case Heathrow Airport should develop weather below our minimum of a quarter-mile visibility on the landing runway.

Our flight time is estimated at only six hours and thirty-two minutes because our normal air speed of 600 mph will be augmented by tail winds of up to 130 mph at some points in our crossing. These jet-stream winds are common on eastbound flights and our routing has been planned to take maximum advantage of them. Incidentally, the fuel that is used for the jet engine closely resembles kerosene with a few impurities removed.

Our 747 weighs more than 750,000 pounds and is

two-thirds as long as a football field. It can carry more than 300,000 pounds of fuel, about 50,000 gallons. Some of the newer 747s have a range of close to 8,000 miles.

Whenever a plane comes in from a flight, a maintenance crew swarms all over it, particularly when it is being prepared for an ocean crossing. While all the essentials plus fuel, oil, and water are checked, a special crew cleans the cabin and another provisions the galley.

Our flight engineer, in the meantime, has gone on out to the aircraft. His preflight check consists first of an exterior inspection—peering into every nook and cranny, examining the tires, struts, wings, tail, fuselage, and flight control surfaces. Then he examines the interior with the same care and precision. His thorough check inside and out takes almost an hour. Before we have even boarded, he has procedurally checked, set, or tested 140 items.

As we leave the dispatch office with our papers, the copilot proceeds to his preflight duties in the cockpit while I go to meet and brief our flight attendants. On a 747, this team comprises up to sixteen flight attendants who will be looking after your safety and comfort. The cabin attendants can add immeasurably to the satisfaction of your flight, and I want to assure them that I, too, as time permits, wish to contribute to this goal. The feeling of a team effort is established. I will also provide them with information on the en route and destination weather.

At least thirty minutes before takeoff, I get settled in the left seat in the cockpit, and we start to go through our extensive checklist. No detail is overlooked. Everything is verified. For instance, when "flap setting" is called out, I reply, "Flap handle set at fifteen degrees, and fifteen degrees shown on indicators."

A takeoff computation sheet has been prepared to show us our acceleration speeds for takeoff and climb. Our jet engines dependably develop so much power that we will use less than half of the runway for takeoff at Kennedy International, and our air speed will continue to accelerate after takeoff even though we will be climbing at an angle of fifteen degrees.

After all the passengers are boarded, and we have completed our preparations to depart, the copilot will call the ground controller for a clearance to taxi to the takeoff runway in use. Even as we start to taxi, there are still over seventy items on the checklist that will be covered before we begin the takeoff roll. I have mentioned the word "check" several times. Today's airline pilot is not the reckless daredevil pilot of wartime fame. We don't take chances. We work as a team, thoroughly checking each gauge and setting, all systems—and each other. We are well trained (and well paid!) professionals.

Let me tell you a little bit about your crew. I've been flying for thirty-five years, including five years of military service during World War II. The copilot and flight engineer probably are ex-service pilots also, with many years of training and experience. The copilot receives the same quality of training as the captain, and captain and copilot usually alternate takeoffs and landings. The flight engineer is usually the junior crewmember as far as seniority is concerned. He is a pilot, but his current training is as a flight engineer. He is our "technical director," monitoring engine performance, fuel consumption, and the electrical, hydraulic, and cabin pressurization systems. He is an integral and important part of the team.

After the control tower has cleared us onto the runway for takeoff, I pick up the microphone and say, "Good evening, this is Captain Cummings. We have been cleared to take off to the southeast. Our flight time to London will be six hours and thirty-two minutes. We anticipate a smooth crossing. I will have more information for you after we have climbed out to our cruising altitude."

I know that some people back there are anxious, and some may be downright scared. Identifying myself and speaking to them in a calm, conversational manner will help put them at ease.

As we roll down the runway, the operation of all our systems is closely observed. If a malfunction were to occur before we reached a determined flying speed, there would be ample room to brake to a stop with close to a mile of runway left over. An engine failure after takeoff does not present a problem either because of the thorough training all the crew has had. (In my thirty years of flying for Pan Am, I can recall having only two engine failures, and both were handled procedurally and routinely.)

After takeoff, we are cleared to "hold runway heading of 130 degrees (almost due southeast) and climb to an altitude of 5,000 feet." Just before reaching that 5,000-foot plateau, we are cleared to turn to a northeast heading and climb to an altitude of 18,000 feet. By now we are about ten miles southeast of the airport, and we are being monitored and guided by Air Traffic Control.

Just before we reach 18,000 feet, we're cleared to climb on-course to our cruising altitude of 35,000 feet.

This means we can now follow our prepared flight plan routing. We are now heading up the northeast coast of the U.S. We will be followed by the radar of Air Traffic Control for the next two hours, until we're 200 miles off the east coast of Newfoundland.

Over land, our main navigational aid is provided by directional radio facilities called VORs (Visual Omni Ranges). There are almost 1,000 in the United States alone. Their locations and frequencies are provided by our navigational charts so that, at a cruising altitude of 35,000 feet, for instance, we can dial the frequency of any station within a 250-mile radius and get a readout that shows us the heading, distance, and time to that station. It sure beats swooping down to read the name of a town off a bank building, as I had to do once in 1942 when, as a second lieutenant, I got lost over the plains of Kansas on a training mission with my bomber crew. One member of my crew was from Kansas, and he was then able to guide me back to Topeka.

At our cruising altitude, seven miles above the earth, the horizon is a long way off. Have you ever watched a sailboat slowly disappear over the horizon a few miles away? In a daytime flight, the line of sight from this altitude to the far horizon is *250* miles. The temperature outside the window is fifty-five degrees below zero, but inside the cabin, it's a comfortable seventy degrees. That cold outside air is compressed by the big jet engines to pressurize our cabin to a comfortable level of about 4,000 feet. The supply and exhaust of cabin air is continuous, and a complete change of air takes about three minutes.

Although we are traveling at 600 miles per hour, you have no awareness of movement unless the plane is accelerating or decelerating. It's quieter than your suburban living room, and the seats are just as comfortable.

After we've passed over Gander, Newfoundland, and flown 200 miles out from the North American mainland, our radar following from Air Traffic Control is discontinued. However, our separation from other aircraft, from now until we approach Heathrow, is fifty miles laterally and 2,000 feet vertically.

The navigational equipment used on these overwater flights is similar to that which unerringly carried our astronauts on the 250,000-mile flight to the moon. It has also guided the Nautilus submarines that have submerged for months and even traveled under the polar ice cap. This precise guidance system provides us with an exact readout of our geographical position (longitude and latitude) above the surface of the earth. The magnetic track and distances between check points are programmed on the ground before takeoff. En route, the system automatically corrects for wind drift. It is an electronic brain that—coupled to our gyros, sensors, and accelerometers—provides us with accuracy in time, track, and distance. This is a completely self-contained unit that requires no assistance from the ground, such as the radio or Loran tracking stations used until a few years ago.

Going eastward toward Europe in winter at night, we can see far to our left, in the polar latitudes, the colorful waving banners of the Northern Lights, Aurora Borealis. It is an unforgettable sight. Returning westward in the daytime, our routing often takes us near the ice-covered land mass of Greenland. Nearby, floating on the deep blue of the ocean, we can often spot huge, snow-white, jagged icebergs that have broken loose from the glacial mass of Greenland. They loom much larger and more distinctly than any ocean liner.

We're far above the clouds, and the air here is smooth. Should we encounter any unusual weather, though, we are well equipped to handle it. Our cockpit radar is used to detect cloud build-ups. Somewhat like the way the beam from the headlights on your car probes the darkness ahead, our electronic radar beams probe the skies up to 250 miles ahead of us. The scope, or range, can be reduced to twenty miles if a closer look is desired. The picture, or profile, is presented to us on a small television screen in the cockpit. You have probably driven into rain storms so intense that you pulled off to the side of the road. Heavy rain doesn't restrict our operation whatsoever because radar tells us what to expect, and possibly avoid, up ahead.

Although this is a comparatively long flight, the time on board seems to pass quickly. The flight attendants serve a full dinner to all the passengers, as well as refreshments. The food served on most airliners today is cooked on the ground by a catering service, quick-frozen, and then reheated in microwave ovens during the flight. Exceptions to the "microwave" rule can often be found in first class, where such delicacies as smoked salmon, caviar, and rare roast beef abound.

Even without these amenities, the time passes quickly because there is something about a long flight, particularly in a jumbo jet, that engenders a congenial atmosphere. As a passenger, I have often had the person next to me confide quite personal thoughts and feelings. We all seem to drop our prejudices and pretenses on a long flight.

Meanwhile, we in the cockpit are occupied but not overly busy. All three of us have routine procedures to attend to—the monitoring of systems, navigation, and the fine tuning of our course headings. But we also have ample time to enjoy our meal. (The flight crew eats from the first-class menu—without the libations, of course!) In observance of an old rule of thumb, each person in the cockpit chooses a different selection on the infinitesimal chance that one of the dishes might cause an upset stomach. The flight attendants look in on us occasionally, and there's often time for a bit of conversation as they serve us food and refreshments. (Incidentally, the cockpit—or flight deck as it is sometimes called—is closed to passengers during flight: it's locked, and only the flight crew and attendants have access to it.)

About two hours out of London, the sun, at first just a faint glow below the horizon, soon appears large and blindingly bright. It's been a short night—five hours shorter than it is back in New York. There is plenty to keep us busy: sending a position report, obtaining weather information, and confirming that our fuel consumption log corresponds to that of our flight plan. Actually, the precision and reliability of today's jet engines give us very accurate figures for our predictable speed and fuel consumption.

The first air traffic controller we talk to after sunrise is at Shannon Airport in Ireland. The Irish have a refreshing lilt to their speech, but their vernacular is quite the same as it is among controllers and pilots the world over—brief and to the point. English has been agreed upon as the official language of flight communication, and it is used whether we are flying into Madrid or Moscow.

Shannon will pick us up on their radar screen some 200 miles out. From that time until we land in London, our position will be monitored. We will, however, continue to follow our planned route unless advised otherwise.

In the meantime, back in the passenger cabin, our flight attendants are completing the breakfast service, stowing equipment, and answering passengers' last-minute questions about things to do and see in London.

Before we begin our descent, I often think about how smoothly, effortlessly, quietly, and accurately we have spanned this vast expanse of water between North America and Europe. During my lifetime, the airplane has evolved from the perilous single-engine novelty of World War I into a huge, safe, comfortable, and speedy transport that daily links the lives and cultures of 2 million inhabitants on our small planet.

London Control has now cleared us for our descent so I again pick up the microphone of the public address system to greet our passengers and inform them of weather conditions, temperature, and estimated time of arrival. The weather below us is cloudy right now, but later, if some distinctive landmarks are visible, I will point them out.

About five minutes before landing, we will begin extending our flaps to slow us down and expedite our descent. The approach controller at Heathrow advises us that it is cloudy and raining at the airport and that the measured visibility of the runway in use is 1,600 feet—well above the minimum for landing. The approach, touchdown, and braking will be accomplished with the use of our autopilot control system.

The approach controller clears us over to the Heathrow tower controller, who answers our call advising us that he has us on his radar screen and that we are clear to land. Nothing is left to chance. All of our navigational and landing approach systems have backups.

Our landing gear is extended, checked, lowered, and locked in place. About one mile out, our landing flaps are fully extended. The checklist is completed, and at a height of about 100 feet above the ground, the lead-in lights of the runway appear, followed by the runway lights themselves. A smooth, completely automated landing is made. Wheel braking is augmented by reversing the engines. A smooth landing, even on autopilot, always provides the pilot with a sense of satisfaction.

As we turn off the landing runway, the tower controller will clear us to the radio frequency of the ground controller, who will direct us in the routing we must use to taxi to the arrival gate.

As our flight attendants are bidding you good-bye, we in the cockpit crew are gathering up our charts and papers. It's seven A.M., and we will not depart London for New York until two o'clock tomorrow afternoon.

I hope this typical flight will ease your uncertainty by providing you with firsthand information about the many ways in which your safety and comfort are assured every step of the way.

CHAPTER VII

PREVENTIVE MAINTENANCE

THE TITLE OF THIS BOOK IS *FREEDOM FROM FEAR OF FLYING*
—and I mean once and for all. Overcoming your fear is
relatively simple once you understand the problem and
decide to do something about it. If you have followed
my suggestions, prepared yourself thoroughly, and
taken a flight or two, you're well over the hump. Now
I'm going to give you some tips on keeping things that
way.

As I've said earlier, you get over the fear of flying by
learning how to fly without fear. It's a skill—or combination of skills—that you practice until the entire
process becomes second nature. Triple A/BM, the
tapes, the relaxation exercises, education about the

nature of flight, and flying itself are all analogous to the various individual movements that together make up a good golf swing. And what holds true for golf, holds true for flying fearlessly: with practice, your skills will continue to improve.

When I am golfing, I notice that many players turn aside any compliment about a difficult shot or a long putt that they have made. Instead, they berate themselves for their inaccuracy on an easier shot earlier in the game. Many fearful flyers display a similar tendency. What they seem to remember best, and repeat often, is the five or ten uncomfortable minutes they might have experienced. Be aware of this tendency and avoid it. Rather, choose to feel some pride about the times during the flight when you were comfortable, sociable, eating, looking out the window, maybe even excited. Remember, choose to starve your fear and feed your progress.

Don't be a perfectionist. Every flight is different. If you fly often, some flights will be better than others. Like anyone else, you may be slightly uncomfortable on a bumpy flight or flying with a cold or when overtired. These are normal responses. Learn not to make too much of it.

Keep aware of all aspects of this course that helped you onto your graduation flight: listen to the tapes, practice the relaxation exercises (you'll find them useful in *any* stressful situation), reread the chapters on the mechanics, physics, and safety of flight—but above all, *fly!*

Fly often, as often as you can. If you fly for business, take more business trips. If you fly for pleasure—on vacations or to visit loved ones—take more trips just

139

for fun. Don't talk yourself out of it because you "don't have the time" or because "it's too expensive." It takes very little time to fly from New York to Boston or Washington, D.C.; from Los Angeles to San Francisco; from Miami to Orlando; and if you plan ahead, those flights can be less expensive today than they have ever been.

Federal deregulation of the airlines in 1978 greatly increased the number of air carriers serving large cities and reduced the service to smaller cities. Through competition for the major markets, deregulation brought about lower prices for air travel. However, long before that, flying had ceased to be the luxurious prerogative of the rich or expense-accounted. Today's low prices have put air travel within most people's reach, especially when compared to the expenses of gas, lodging, and food when driving. The two-hour-and-twenty-minute flight from New York to Miami equals three days of driving time. But lower air fares also mean fewer frills, and if you are naïve about scheduling and pricing, you can end up bewildered and frustrated. For instance, it is estimated that there are 8,000 changes in air fares every month. Advance planning is essential to secure a reserved seat on the airline of your choice.

Here are some things you can do to make flying serve your needs. The major airlines often publish some of their schedules and fares in newspaper ads. A monthly publication called the OAG (Official Airline Guide) will provide you with information about connecting flights and their schedules. A telephone call to the individual airlines will give you information about their service and fares. However, the best overall picture may be obtained through a travel agent. Find one you like and trust. They can give you a wide choice of airlines, times, and prices. And buying your ticket from a travel agent doesn't cost any more than when waiting in a long line to buy it at the airport.

Become a bit of a "buff" on fares and schedules. Recall how learning about the mechanics of your phobia made you feel more hopeful of overcoming it. Knowledge is power—it pushes back the darkness of ignorance. In the same way, new facts about air safety have made you more secure about flying. In fact, you are now in a position to correct others' misconceptions about the airline industry. If you continue to educate yourself about flying today—about the different manufacturers and models, new designs, special benefits for frequent flyers—this knowledge will make you feel even more in control. If possible, make friends with people in the airline industry and ask them about their work.

Now that you have overcome your own fear, be on the lookout for others who are fearful when flying. Statistics tell us that one in six flyers are afraid to some degree. As a *former* fearful flyer you are in the best position to be empathetic and supportive. Reaching out to a fearful flyer will also reinforce your own progress and make you feel better.

Continue to introduce yourself to flight crews and tell them of overcoming your fear. This sometimes results in a better seat or better service. Continue to engage yourself in the experience of flight. Look out the window; learn about different cloud formations. Listen to the pilot's announcements of particularly impressive views.

Rejoice in the sorts of things that flying allows you to do. After all, flying is a means to an end. Consider how to help it enhance your life. Expand your career or your knowledge of different places and cultures through flying. You are now *free* to do any of these things.

The ability to fly can change your entire life if you let it. Flying is a way of life in the late 20th century. Let it be *your* way of life as you leave your old fears and limitations farther and farther behind.

CHAPTER VIII

HEALTH IN FLIGHT
(Tips for Flying Comfortably)

I am concerned about airsickness. Can you give me some information?

I can give you some information based on my experience. Scientists are not in agreement as to the cause. My opinion is that the motion sickness of flight is caused by the emotion sickness of fear. With one exception, I know of no one who, after completing one of my seminars or using the relaxation tapes, has suffered from airsickness. The exception occurred on a hot summer day in Philadelphia when our graduation flight was delayed more than two hours with a maintenance problem. It was still hot after we became airborne, and one woman—seemingly quite unconcerned—made use of her "burp bag." I distinctly remember the incident because her brief, mild distress was far outweighed by her smiling satisfaction at being aloft.

You can minimize the small chance of getting airsick by eating lightly on the day of your flight and by avoiding coffee or liquor. There are antinausea drugs available, but remember that these may have side effects—such as light-headedness, mild disorientation, or mild depression—that will interfere with your ability to perform the relaxation exercises. Try flying without these drugs. If you find that you really need something, see your doctor and explain the *whole* problem, including your fear, rather than grabbing something over the counter.

During the descent and landing, my eardrums bother me. Sometimes it is barely noticeable. Other times it is painful. What can I do?

The discomfort you experience is caused by the increase of atmospheric pressure against the sensitive eardrum as you descend. Modern aircraft are pressurized so that those changes are minimized. The American Council on Otolaryngology, in a pamphlet published as a public service, recommends that you chew gum or melt mints in your mouth just before and during descent. Many people find that simply swallowing will do the trick. Yawning is even better. It stretches the muscles that can open the pressure block in the eustachian tube. If yawning and swallowing are not effective, the most forceful way to unblock your ears is: 1. Pinch your nostrils shut. 2. Take a mouthful of air. 3. Using your cheek and throat muscles, force the air to the back of your nose as if you were trying to blow your thumb and fingers off of your nostrils. When you hear a pop in your ear, you will have succeeded. You may have to repeat this several times during the descent. (Not recommended for those with colds or sinus problems!)

If your discomfort is severe and occurs every time you fly, see your doctor. If medication is prescribed, make sure it is mild, explaining about your fear of flying and your concern about side effects to your doctor. Stay awake during the descent so that you can combat ear pressure with the exercises. If you've arrived at the point where you're comfortable enough to sleep in flight, congratulations! Ask your neighbor to wake you up during the descent, though.

I have always been afraid that my fear, especially during takeoff, might cause me to hyperventilate. Isn't hyperventilation dangerous?

No. Hyperventilation can be precipitated by fear, and its onset is indicated by short and rapid breathing. It is frightening because it occurs involuntarily. The exaggerated breathing produces an excess of oxygen and a depletion of carbon dioxide in the bloodstream, which could cause a harmless light-headed or dizzy feeling. You needn't worry about it, however, because by *voluntarily* initiating the deep breathing process, you will prevent the *involuntary* response of hyperventilation. Triple A/BM will stop hyperventilation as well as other symptoms associated with rising fear.

Don't a lot of fearful flyers overdrink before getting on the plane?

Yes, and as I've pointed out, it usually works as a handicap rather than a help. This conclusion has come

145

from the people who finally started flying sober because booze wasn't helping.

Others I have worked with told me that they finally had to quit flying because their excess consumption of liquor, before and during a flight, seemed to be leading them to alcoholism. Another man, a very moderate drinker, overdrank on a flight and blacked out. He awakened the next morning unaware of what city or what hotel he was in and found out that he had disembarked at an intermediate stop several hundred miles short of his destination. Let me repeat that the drugs taken to avoid the feeling experience of flight will only serve to intensify the threat.

CHAPTER IX

FORMER FEARFUL FLYERS SPEAK OUT

THIS IS A SELECTION OF LETTERS FROM *FORMER* FEARFUL flyers. See if you can find one that fits your experience.

Friendswood, Texas
Dear Slim,

I can fly! Sweet exodus from the nest that I so carefully and comfortably arranged. Bon voyage to the harbor I built to imprison my very soul. Off, off I go to experience my feelings as I experience the world around me. All because I met my fear, and discovered that it was just a feeling. And after allowing that feeling to run its course through me, I realized that fear becomes impotent when it is accepted and felt as a feeling. As long as I locked my fear up, it would threaten me and beat on the door. I opened the door and found a pussycat.

You helped me to locate my courage to open that door. Thank you for being who you are and for caring about what happens to me.

Houston, Texas
Dear Slim,

As you will remember, prior to the Fearful Flyers seminar I had not been able to force myself to get on an airplane for fifteen years. During the past twelve months, I have flown 65,000 miles.

The only bad experience I had on any of my trips occurred the day before Thanksgiving. Flying standby from Denver to Houston, I had to sit in the nonsmoking section and for a confirmed nicotine addict, that was torture. (I guess that should be my next self-improvement campaign.)

Seriously, I have gone from a "fearful flyer" to a "joyous flyer"; some of my most relaxful and peaceful moments these days are spent on an airplane.

This is especially interesting when you consider that when I woke up on the morning of our graduation flight, I was so frightened of the prospect of flying I had no intention of going, but decided to go to the airport to see the rest of the group off. Obviously I did go, but I must confess I took enough money to ride the train back if necessary.

On the first flight by myself I was mildly apprehensive on the way to the airport, but the trip was fantastic. Then, on my first trip to London, there was the same mild apprehension because I had not been on a flight over two hours long and that one was to be nine hours; but other than being slightly boring, it was great.

Since then it all has been great. In fact, I just returned from vacations in Europe which neither my family nor I could ever have experienced without your assistance.

New Caney, Texas
Dear Slim,
    I thought you might find my itinerary for the past year interesting (for a former fearful flyer):

February	Tulsa
	London
March	Mexico City
	New York
April	Mexico City
	Lima, Peru
	Buenos Aires
	São Paulo
	Rio de Janeiro
July	Mexico City
	Sydney, Australia
August	Perth, Australia
September	Montreal
October	London
	Mexico City
November	Washington, D.C.
	New Orleans
	Tulsa
December	London

New Bedford, Massachusetts
Dear Slim,
    Last week when I flew to Chicago, and again this week when I flew back, I thought of you and how much you changed my life last year. As I sat and looked out the

window, I thought of the many times I had taken a train or driven on similar trips in the eight years I didn't fly because of my fear.

I was so relaxed that when we experienced a little bumpiness, I calmed my wife down. Isn't that something —me, the guy who used to be so afraid.

Gaithersburg, Maryland
Dear Slim,

I think of you often, my friend, but especially on the ninth of May. Three years ago today, I became a Former Fearful Flyer by sharing some tears and laughter with a wonderful group of people as we flew from Baltimore to Atlantic City and back. I had flown before, but it always terrified me. I had spent the last two years being too afraid to get on an airplane at all. I can't tell you the relief I felt. Oh, I was still scared, but you had taught me that it was okay to be afraid and that I could deal with it. I have been flying—and feeling progressively more comfortable and less afraid—ever since. I've even slept on an airplane—something I never dreamed possible.

Less than a year after my graduation flight, I was promoted to General Sales Manager—a position that requires a lot of flying. Since then, my job has taken me all over the United States, and to Canada and England as well. Today, I truly enjoy flying. I know all the airplanes and all the airlines. I ask for window seats so I can see the view. I eat, drink, and yes, I even take a nap once in a while. There's an additional benefit to being a Former Fearful Flyer—you meet some very nice people. Every now and then I notice someone doing relaxation exercises before takeoff and wiggling their toes before the takeoff roll, or they notice me. The next thing I know, I have a new friend.

I must tell you one more thing. With a recent trip to Houston, I have accumulated over 90,000 miles on Continental's Frequent Flyer Program. That means my wife and I will be flying to Hawaii and Australia this winter for free! Pretty good for a guy too scared to get on an airplane three years ago, wouldn't you say? It sure feels good to be free of an irrational fear that has controlled my life.

Annandale, Virginia
Dear Captain Cummings,

I just returned from a nine-day trip to Reno and Houston via Chicago and Denver. We had a total of twelve takeoffs and landings, five of which were in rain, three in snow, and the final one in the heavy winds that buffeted National Airport on Sunday and capsized approximately fifty sailboats. I want you to know that thanks to you, I was the calmest person on the plane.

I would like to offer my volunteer services as living, walking proof that your wonderful program works. Prior to your course, I had to get stone drunk to step aboard a plane, and since I quit drinking seven years ago, I would not fly. I now look forward to many trips to all parts of the world.

Florham Park, New Jersey
Dear Slim,

I wanted to write to you sooner, but I have just returned from vacation. I thought you might be interested in knowing how my life has changed as a result of your class.

I am delighted to say that my fear of flying is now conquered 100 percent. Since attending your class seven months ago, I have been on a total of eleven flights.

FREEDOM FROM FEAR OF FLYING

I believe this is quite an accomplishment for someone who walked off an airplane with an anxiety attack approximately ten years ago. In the years to follow I was petrified even at the thought of getting on an airplane.

On our graduation flight to Boston it was very difficult for me to board the plane. However, many people may find this hard to believe, but when the plane left the ground in Newark, I knew my problem would soon be solved.

Working for Dun & Bradstreet, I have had many opportunities in the past to travel. Unfortunately, I was always unable to take advantage of these trips because of my fear of flying. I finally enrolled in your class so I could attend a special Presentation Citation Awards meeting for my company in Palm Springs, California. Not only did I attend the meeting, but I actually fell asleep on the return flight home.

Because of you, I feel a great deal better about myself, as I have defeated a fear that had plagued me for many years. This has also given me more confidence in other areas of my life.

At the present time, reflecting upon my experience, I can honestly say that I envy the people who will participate in your class and follow your instructions. They will undoubtedly experience the same wonderful change in their lives as I have in my own.

Indianapolis, Indiana
Dear Slim,

Here is a letter from a member of the "little seminar" held in Cleveland last October. I was the fellow who drove up from Columbus, Ohio (140 miles), and whose wife was about to undergo open-chest surgery. When I came to see you, I had been afraid to get on an airplane

152

for over eight years, and was so ashamed of myself that I lived in dread that my professional associates might find out about my fear. I went to great lengths to arrange my business trips by train, car, or bus (avoiding, of course, overseas travel, which no doubt hurt me professionally), and to keep those arrangements secret as far as possible. Vacation possibilities were also quite limited.

How much I learned from you! From your examples, your support, your training in the use of the tools, and the opportunity you provided me to get to know others with similar fears, I finally learned how to handle my fear. I remember clearly that beautiful day of our graduation flight, how much we all supported each other, how warm and human an experience it was.

And here I am, four months, fourteen airplanes, and 8,000 air miles later. I wouldn't have believed it possible! Six days after graduation, I flew "solo" (by U.S. Air) to New York on business, and came back the next day. What a great feeling! Since then I have been on a plane trip at least once a month—to Chicago, to Florida, to California. Each flight has been a new learning experience. The best, so far, was when my wife (recovered from surgery and doing fine), my two children, and I all flew together to Florida for a Christmas-time vacation. During the flight I commented to my wife that it was the first time the four of us had ever flown somewhere together just for fun. I remember what a pleasant surprise it was when, on one leg of that trip, we discovered that our aircraft was a wide-body—an L1011 Tristar. That was the best flight yet; I was actually sorry to see it end!

I find, although I can remember my old fears, that I need to use the tools less as time goes by; it really does get easier. I enjoy walking around a plane in flight, and it has its special rewards: "circumnavigating" a crowded 747 on the way to Los Angeles, I ran into two people I knew! I find I can let go more—trust the scheduling completely to a travel agent, enjoy a meal in flight, even get on a plane delayed three hours for "mechanical difficulties" a few days after that Eastern airliner's belly landing in Miami. What confidence you instill!

My wife and I are now planning a combination business/vacation trip to Europe this summer. We expect to visit France, Switzerland, Germany, and Belgium, and we don't expect to go by ship (nice, but too expensive).

Houston, Texas
Dear Slim,

It's been six months since I attended your seminar in Houston, and I've intended to write ever since. But I'm glad I procrastinated because much has happened during the last six months—important and positive things that I believe are directly related to the time I spent with you. I thought you might like to receive a progress report, tardy though it is.

I flew to Colorado two weeks after the seminar. I anticipated the trip with just a little bit less than my usual amount of apprehension. At first I was disappointed, but somewhere en route, I realized that I was almost enjoying certain aspects of the flight—watching the excitement my son felt, experiencing the sense of adventure that for so long I had let fear overshadow. For me, then, it became clear that 95 percent of my problem was preflight and not actual on-the-plane discomfort. I also recognized that just making the decision to try to overcome my fear did more for my self-esteem than anything I had ever done before. Taking charge, being in control, was so much more important than I had realized. Anticipating a flight filled me with the same old feeling of dread.

Then one day in November, a friend called me from New York to ask if I would meet her and her son at Disney World—the next day. I said I'd let her know. During the next hour I thought and thought and couldn't come up with one reason (besides my fear) not to go. I knew it would be good for me, and fun, so . . . I called her back and said yes. I took the trip and had one of the best times of my life. Since it was a spur-of-the-moment, impulsive decision, I eliminated the preflight worry period—I didn't have time to think about all the terrible things that could happen. Without having gone through the apprehension, I actually enjoyed the excitement of the flight and was able to look forward to the fun I would have once there, rather than dwelling on the misery of getting there. That trip proved to me that vacations don't have to be ruined by fear and apprehension.

A few weeks after that trip, my husband started pushing for a winter trip to Colorado. I then gave a lot of thought to all you said about fearful flyers setting up patterns of avoidance, and I realized that I was a perfect case in point. So I decided to go to Colorado just so as not to avoid flying. I'm writing you now from this winter wonderland in the Rockies. I flew here with less apprehension than ever before. What's even more remarkable than my learning to be a comfortable flyer is that I've found that I'm starting to take control over many other areas of my life. And I believe that I owe this change to you, for your practical explanations and positive approach to us and our problem, and for the warmth and understanding you had during a most intense and emotional time. I was deeply impressed with your genuine concern for all of us. And I thank you.

P.S. I'd like to add that I use the relaxation techniques you showed us, and I find them very helpful in all kinds of stressful situations. I intend to use them lots next September when my entire family goes to Africa on a photographic safari.

Canton, Ohio
Dear Captain Cummings,

I wanted to take this opportunity to express to you some of the thoughts and experiences that I have had since I first contacted you for assistance.

My first opportunity to fly came in the summer of 1965, when I was seventeen years old, and boarded a United Airlines twin engine, propeller-driven plane for a flight to Chicago. The excitement and enthusiasm I felt before, during, and after the flight was almost indescribable. I loved every minute of it. In the next several years, I had the opportunity to fly several times a year and viewed each experience as an enjoyable one.

In 1970, I flew direct from Cleveland to Los Angeles. During the four-and-one-half-hour flight to California, we did experience some rather severe turbulence. It was the first time I had experienced such severe turbulence on a flight, and I was somewhat uneasy. In looking back, I doubt that we were ever in any type of danger, but I don't think I felt so at the time. At the time that the turbulence was encountered, a meal was being served, and the jolting and shaking of trays and food was extremely unpleasant.

The following year, I flew, but I was extremely nervous, due in large part, I believe, to the experiences a *year earlier. I do seem to recall that on that flight, I resolved that this whole process may not be as safe as I thought and that it might be some time before I would fly again. In the next ten years, I did not have the opportunity to fly again, and certainly did not go out of my way to make an opportunity.*

For several months prior to May of 1983, my family had been planning a trip to Philadelphia for the purpose of attending my younger sister's graduation from graduate school. As the time to depart grew closer, I became more anxious. On the night before the flight, I was extremely uncomfortable and had a great deal of difficulty eating and sleeping. The next morning I contacted the airline and canceled my reservations. It was the first time in my life that I had avoided a flight. It was a morning that I shall never forget and I truly believe that the feelings that I experienced that day played a large part in my desire to rectify the situation.

As I was packing to drive to Philadelphia, I became so overwhelmed with my feelings of depression and felt so distraught that I became physically sick to my stomach. I drove the ten hours, making only one stop for gasoline, and was terribly depressed the entire time.

After I returned home, I made a commitment to myself that something would be done. One of the first places I went upon my return was the public library, where I began researching the literature for materials on the fear of flying and phobic flyers. One name that kept reappearing in the journals and literature was yours and specifically your program. I read about how you had worked with people and how they had been helped. I felt new hope.

Over the next four or five months, I frequently listened to my tapes and read the books. Late in July, I received a call from a friend of mine who invited me to his wedding, which was going to be held in September outside of New York City. It seemed as though someone was trying to tell me that this was my opportunity. As the time neared for the journey, I became somewhat uneasy but your words of advice and conditioning gave me comfort and strength. One of the strongest points that I kept thinking about was your statement that an avoidance of the flight experience only serves to make the situation worse. I had experienced one avoidance and was determined not to experience another.

In September of 1983, my friend and I flew to Newark. It was a pleasant flight, and while I was uncomfortable, I tolerated the experience. I had a tremendous feeling of satisfaction and accomplishment and a true sense of indebtedness to you and your program. I had been able to face the experience and succeed, although not as comfortably as I would have liked.

It is difficult for me to express in words how much your program has meant to me. I don't know why my attitude about flying changed from sheer delight to fear for whatever reason it did. However, your program gave me the courage and faith to confront the problem. I think there are many reasons why your program has helped, not the least of which is your background. I felt a confidence in you due to the fact that you speak not only as a psychologist who has studied the phenomenon but also as an experienced airline pilot. That combination of pilot/psychologist is a most comforting one.

I am deeply grateful that there was a ray of hope amidst all of the darkness of fear and frustration. Every step that I take is taken with your help and guidance.

Again, my deepest and most sincere thanks. You and your program serve a vital function for thousands of people. Best of luck with your efforts.

Houston, Texas
Dear Slim,

I am sure that it isn't often that you hear a complaint from the spouse of one of your FFF-ers. The truth is that since Liz took your course, I haven't been able to keep her home. First it was Rome with the FFF group, then the Yucatan, later New Orleans, then three weeks in the Holy Land and right after that Seattle. You can see that I'm considering having her deprogrammed.

Of course, I'm only kidding because your program has brought a remarkable change in our lives and in our traveling. . . . Keep up the good work.

Yonkers, New York
Dear Slim,

I am taking time from my busy schedule to thank you for changing my lifestyle and for opening so many doors to new horizons for me.

My son moved to Denver two years ago. I have just returned from there and actually enjoyed the flight.

The fear I dreaded never happened! How grateful I am to you, along with my entire family, for making this trip possible. In addition to being able to make the flight, I also drove through the tunnel in the Rocky Mountains. No one would believe that after thirty-five years of claustrophobia, this would happen.

I have spent much money and time during the past twenty years trying to cure my fear to no avail until I was fortunate enough to find your program.

FREEDOM FROM FEAR OF FLYING

Findlay, Ohio
Dear Slim,

I am dictating this while I am driving back home following our trip, because I wanted you to have the benefits of our thoughts while they were so fresh from our experience together. I must start by telling you that I have a feeling of inner peace that has seldom been matched in my lifetime. Some of that, I know, comes from the pride of accomplishment. Some of it has come from the realization that I have finally found a vehicle which will help me get this monkey off my back. Some of it has come from a feeling of shared experience with our little group and, finally, but not in any way the least— and perhaps even the most—some of it is due to having known you.

You have given us many gifts in the last couple of days. Certainly you have shown us a way toward freedom from the burden that we were carrying. In my case, you have also given me the possibility to look at life differently in the future, to experience more joyously the sensations and opportunities of life that are all around us.

I want to convey to you my deepest thanks for what Slim Cummings and his program have done for me.

CHAPTER X

FURTHER THOUGHTS

Two caterpillars were inching their way through the grass when a butterfly fluttered perilously overhead. They looked up in awe. One caterpillar nudged the other and said: "You couldn't get me up in one of those things for a million dollars!"

MANKIND HAS ALWAYS BEEN AWED AND INTRIGUED BY the mystery of flight. The skies have always beckoned to us. The inaccessible heavens have always been a symbol of power, divinity, omnipotence. Early man's awe and wonder was tempered by the threatening gods of thunder and lightning.

Ancient civilizations restricted flying to the gods. The Romans' messenger of god was Mercury, with wings on his helmet, feet, and wand. The Greeks had their symbol of celestial power and speed in Pegasus, the winged horse. The early Christians deified those who were selected to ascend to heaven by giving them wings and calling them angels.

Man has been unceasing in his quest to conquer the skies. Leonardo da Vinci made more than a thousand drawings of how flight might be accomplished. He drew kites, parachutes, balloons, and helicopters. His "flappable" wings were designed to be attached to a man's arms. Efforts to emulate the birds resulted in a lot of busted heads and broken bones.

More than 200 years ago, in France, the first experiments were made with balloons. First, a smoke-filled bag was sent aloft. It rose because smoke contains hot air, and hot air rises. In 1783, a large cloth bag, thirty-five feet in diameter, was filled with hot air and released. It drifted a few miles before it descended to earth. It was immediately attacked by frightened farmers who pierced it with pitchforks.

Soon the hot air for balloons was furnished by burning charcoal placed on a pan attached beneath the bag. In a demonstration for His Highness, King Louis XVI, a carrying basket was improvised, and a duck, a rooster, and a sheep were put inside it. The flight lasted eight minutes, and all aboard landed unharmed.

Later a balloon carrying two valiant men ascended to an altitude of 500 feet and drifted over Paris for twenty-five minutes. In Philadelphia, in 1793, a large crowd, honored by the presence of President George Washington, viewed the spectacular ascent of a manned balloon.

Next came gliders, some fixed like the wings of a giant bird—but "unflappable." They could glide downhill on a cushion of air like a skier gliding down a cushion of snow. Others were shaped like open-ended boxes. In the late 1800s, the Wright brothers (two bicycle mechanics from Ohio) experimented with gliders.

The locomotive, the telephone, and the gas engine had already been put to use by the time the Wright brothers, on December 17, 1903, filled the world with wonder when they made the first powered flight off a lonely, windswept beach in Kitty Hawk, North Carolina. The flight covered 120 feet and lasted ten seconds.

The world has not been the same since.

There are more than one million people living in America today who were alive when the Wright brothers dared to defy gravity in that first powered air machine. Now, almost one million people defy gravity every day in the United States alone, and proceed safely and surely to destinations at an average distance of 1,000 miles. Although we are still impressed with the audacity of flight, the thunder of takeoffs, and the gentleness of speed and power, these very wonders have established today's jet aircraft as the ultra-safe method of transportation.

The aim of this book has been to enable you to combine your innate yearning to fly and your resistance to the experience of flight—to blend your feelings of awe and intrigue with your feelings of threat and fear.

Miracles happen when people shed fear. They blossom. I've seen many people who, once freed from fear, look younger, stand taller, and come alive with more energy and confidence. Every facet of their life changes favorably—and other fears and anxieties diminish.

Esteem is often equated with the way other people regard you. But much more important, maybe next to life itself, is the way you regard yourself. Overcoming your fear of flying will add a new quality to your life—revitalize your self-esteem.

For years I have been privileged to share the experience of achievement with those who choose to confront their "bully." It is inspiring and encouraging for me to play a part in this beauty and excitement. I thank you

for the opportunity to be your guide in finding your
freedom from fear.

Most of the following quotations have been furnished
by former fearful flyers. They have helped me and
many others in times of doubt and fear. Pick up this
book and flip it to this section whenever you feel like
it. There will always be a saying here that applies to
you.

Fear & Courage

To continue to live with your fear is to confine
yourself in a self-made prison. If a man harbors any
sort of fear, it percolates through all of his thinking, damages his personality, makes him landlord
to the ghost.

—Lloyd Douglas

The fear of danger is ten times more terrifying than
the danger itself.

—Daniel Defoe, *Robinson Crusoe*

There is no disgrace in being afraid.
The only disgrace is yielding to fear.

—Elbert Hubbard

The mind is its own place, and in itself
Can make a Heaven of Hell, a Hell of Heaven.

—Milton, *Paradise Lost*

The only thing we have to fear is fear itself.

—Franklin D. Roosevelt,
Inaugural Address, March 1933

I have a faint cold fear thrills through my veins,
That almost freezes up the heat of life.

—Shakespeare, *Romeo and Juliet*

No one would ever have crossed the ocean if he could have gotten off the ship during the storm.

—Charles F. Kettering

Fear makes men ready to believe the worst. Do the thing you fear and the extinction of that fear is certain.

—Emerson

The worst sorrows in life are not in its losses and misfortune, but its fears.

—A. C. Benson

The one permanent emotion of the inferior man is fear—fear of the unknown, the complex, the inexplicable. What he wants beyond everything is safety.

—H. L. Mencken

Fear is an insidious virus. Given a breeding place in our minds, it will permeate the whole body of our work; it will eat away our spirit and block the forward path of our endeavors. Fear is the greatest enemy of progress. Progress moves ever on, and does not linger to consider microscopically the implications of each particular action. Only in small and overcautious minds are the shadows of lurking enemies and dangers everywhere . . . Fear is met and destroyed with courage. Again and again, when the struggle seems hopeless and all opportunity lost—some man or woman with a little more courage, a little more effort, brings victory.

—James F. Bell

Nothing splendid has ever been achieved except by those who dared believe that something inside them was superior to circumstance.

—Bruce Barton

Nothing in life is to be feared.
It is only to be understood.

—Marie Curie

The proper course with every kind of fear is to think about it rationally and calmly—until it has become completely familiar. In the end, familiarity will blunt its terrors. A fear which we are unwilling to face grows worse by not being looked at.

—Bertrand Russell

All the problems become smaller if you don't dodge them, but confront them. Touch a thistle timidly, and it pricks you; grasp it boldly, and its spines crumble.

—Admiral William S. Halsey

Certainty

Perhaps to a limited extent we can undo what has been done to us and what we have done to ourselves . . . [but first] we have to realize that we are as deeply afraid to live and to love as we are to die.

—R. D. Laing

The desire for safety stands against every great and noble enterprise.

—Tacitus

On learning to ride a flying machine, if you are looking for perfect safety, you will do well to sit on a fence and watch the birds. But if you wish to learn, you must mount a machine and become acquainted with its tricks by actual trial.

—Wilbur Wright, 1901

We cannot have absolute certainty but we must find dependable ways of discerning different degrees of probability. The child in us demands certainty. The adult can accept the fact that there is not always certainty.

—Thomas Harris, M.D., *I'm OK—You're OK*

There is no such thing as security. There has never been.

—Germaine Greer

Nothing will ever be attempted if all possible objections must first be overcome.

—Anonymous

Only the insecure strive for security.

—Anonymous

Change

It is an idiocy to assume that anyone can be alive and not be changing constantly. There are many who go through the years without changing, but they are the ones who huddle on a chronological treadmill searching for an illusionary security and something called *status*. The senility of security and status afflicts many of the so-called young. They never live. Life is an adventure of passion, risk, danger, laughter, beauty, love, a burning curiosity to go with the action to see what it is all about, to search for a pattern of meaning, to burn one's bridges because you're never going back anyway, and to live to the end. Terrified by this dramatic vista, most people just exist; they turn from the turbulence of change and try to hide in their private make-believe harbors, called, in politics, conservatism; in the church, prudence; and in everyday life, *being sensible*.

—Saul Alinsky

Seize this very minute;
What you can do or dream
You can do, begin it;
Boldness has genius, power
And magic in it.
Only engage and then the
Mind grows heated;
Begin and the work will
be completed.

—Goethe

We are told that talent creates its own opportunities. But it sometimes seems that intense desire not only creates its own opportunities, but its own talents.

—Eric Hoffer

Indecision is fatal. It is better to make a wrong decision than build up a habit of indecision. If you're wallowing in indecision, you certainly can't act—and action is the basis of success.

—Marie Beynon Ray

To try and fail is at least to learn; to fail to try is to suffer the inestimable loss of what might have been.

—Chester Barnard

It is the loss of the freedom to change that marks the onset of neurotic behavior.

—Dr. Fritz Perls

It is always safe to assume, not that the old way is wrong, but that there might be a better way.

—Henry R. Harrower

One Day at a Time

There are two days in every week about which we should not worry: two days which should be kept free from fear and apprehension.

One of those days is yesterday, with its mistakes and cares, its faults and blunders, its aches and pains. Yesterday has passed forever beyond our control! All the money in the world cannot undo a single act we performed; we cannot erase a single word said . . . yesterday is gone!

The other day we need not worry about is tomorrow, with its possible burdens, its large promise and poor performance. Tomorrow is also beyond our immediate control. Tomorrow's sun will rise, either in splendor or behind a mask of clouds . . . but it will rise. Until it does, we have no stake in tomorrow. For it is yet unborn.

This leaves only one day . . . today. Any man can fight the battle of just one day . . . it is only when you and I have the burdens in those two awful eternities . . . yesterday and tomorrow . . . that we break down.

It is not the experience of today that drives me mad . . . it is the remorse or bitterness for something which happened yesterday and the dread of what tomorrow may bring.

Let us, therefore, live but *one day at a time*.

—Alcoholics Anonymous

If I had my life to live over, I'd dare to make more mistakes next time. I'd relax, I would limber up. I would be sillier than I have been this trip. I would take fewer things seriously. I would take more chances. I would climb more mountains and swim more rivers. I would eat more ice cream and less beans. I would perhaps have more actual troubles, but I'd have fewer imaginary ones.

You see, I'm one of those people who live sanely and sensibly hour after hour, day after day. Oh, I've had my moments, and if I had it to do over again, I'd have more of them. In fact, I'd try to have nothing else. Just moments, one after another, instead of living so many years ahead of each day. I've been one of those persons who never goes anywhere without a thermometer, a hot water bottle, a raincoat, and a parachute. If I had to do it again, I would travel lighter than I have.

If I had my life to live over, I would start barefoot earlier in the spring and stay that way later in the fall. I would go to more dances. I would ride more merry-go-rounds. I would pick more daisies.

—Nadine Stair (written when she was eighty-five years old)

Flying

Capture a sunset, ride with the wind,
Taste freedom only the eagle has known.
For yours is the freedom of knowing
You have flown.

—Barbara Shaw Jameson

High Flight

Oh! I have slipped the surly bonds of earth,
  And danced the skies on laughter-silvered wings;
Sunward I've climbed, and joined the tumbling mirth
  Of sun-split clouds—and done a hundred things
You have not dreamed of—wheeled and soared
    and swung
  High in the sunlit silence. Hov'ring there,
I've chased the shouting wind along, and flung
  My eager craft through footless halls of air.
Up, up the long, delirious, burning blue
  I've topped the windswept heights with easy
    grace,
Where never lark, or even eagle flew.
  And while with silent, lifting mind I've trod
The high untrespassed sanctity of space,
  Put out my hand and touched the face of God.
                    —John Gillespie Magee Jr.
    Flight Lieutenant, Royal Canadian Air Force

CHAPTER XI

AN OPEN LETTER TO THE U.S. AIR-TRAVEL INDUSTRY

IT IS SAD BUT TRUE THAT THE AIR-TRAVEL INDUSTRY WOULD prefer to ignore the cause of the fearful flyer. They are even reluctant to admit the problem. The president of one large airline, whom I introduced myself to as we were both awaiting a boarding time, said: "Oh, are there still people out there who are afraid to fly?" When I wrote to the president of another airline, he referred me to the Air Transport Association, who in turn said it was a matter for the airlines. . . .

All of this vigorous inactivity continues even though the 25 million fearful flyers in the U.S. alone represent literally billions of dollars in lost revenue. (According to the Boeing Company, one out of six American adults is afraid to fly, although not all are full-fledged phobics.

They make two-thirds fewer flights than those who are unafraid, costing the airline industry an estimated $1.6 billion annually in lost revenue.)

The suggestions that follow are adapted from my own response to a survey by Boeing designed to find ways to combat the problem of fearful flyers. I commend their effort highly (as I commend Pan Am, which has cooperated with me in all my endeavors to help fearful flyers), and I hope that these suggestions are heeded.

Industry Assistance to Treatment Programs: Fewer than one out of five fearful flyers will ever even consider attending a treatment program. The top management resistance that I have encountered was largely due to a lack of understanding of the problem and what to do about it. The industry will continue to resist any association with a "treatment" program but they may well consider an approach that's "educational."

Direct Industry Action: The Public Broadcasting Service (PBS) would probably be very interested in showing a first-rate educational film that presents a simple explanation of how a big B-747 gets off the ground, how the jet engine works, and how the many backup systems help to assure a safe and comfortable flight.

The airlines—even in a combined project—could sponsor regular aircraft familiarization tours with selected uniformed cockpit and cabin crews and mechanics in attendance. A well-publicized local flight of one hour's duration would fill up at a "cost" price of $20 a head.

In-Flight Provisions: The one thing that I would like to see started without further delay is what Boeing mentions as a "specially designed brochure for the back

173

of the seat pocket": information presented to reassure the fearful flyer need not be much different from that of general interest. Also, one of the channels of the on-board audio systems could carry a sequence of procedures to coincide with start-up, taxi, takeoff, etc. All long flights should carry a selection for a relaxation tape. An informational booklet about the fear of flying and how it can be somewhat allayed should, at least, be available to all personnel who come in contact with passengers—including cockpit crews.

In the meantime pilots should be made aware that there are always anxious flyers on board. They should make the small extra effort it takes to get on the public address system during turbulence, holding patterns, and other potentially frightening situations to reassure the passengers that nothing dangerous is happening.

Training in this area has long been neglected for flight attendants and cockpit crews. All should be made aware that the anxious flyer becomes even more anxious when delays at the gate, before takeoff, and before landing are unexplained. Public address announcements are sometimes carelessly or inaudibly presented, and sometimes use shocking terms such as "severe turbulence," "emergency," "terminal," "engine loss," "*final* approach."

Advertising: The airlines spend hundreds of millions on advertising each year, pushing friendly service, special fares, frequent flyer awards, wide-bodied accommodations, and so on. Regular travelers might be lured with this pitch, but none of it holds any appeal to the fearful flyer. Most are too fearful even to consider a trip in a plane. If the airlines would only consider allotting just 5 percent of their advertising budget to a public service program of help to the millions and millions grounded by their fear, they would certainly see a much better return on their money.

Future Work: More work needs to be done to assess and improve the help now available to fearful flyers. This can be best accomplished by increasing the amount, and enhancing the quality, of help available to them at present. I suggest that the air transportation industry (possibly the Air Transport Association) consider organizing the people who work with fearful flyers. This effort would bring the individuals and programs thinly scattered at present together, enabling them to agree on guidelines for appropriate treatment as well as increasing public awareness of its availability. The organization could also supply information about films, tours, self-help groups, materials, and knowledgeable leadership.

The people who are in closest contact with the fearful passenger are the cabin flight attendants. Let's get a survey questionnaire out to a sampling of these people. How frequently do they notice fear? What do they do about it? Are they taught, in their training, what to do? What are their concerns? What are their recommendations?

Answers to these and other questions, and firm action on the suggestions proposed, would help a significant portion of the American population in an unprecedented gesture of enlightened self-interest by the U.S. air-travel industry.

APPENDIX

REPORT ON THE FREEDOM FROM FEAR OF FLYING SEMINARS

The following is adapted from Understanding Phobias: Evaluation of an Aviophobia Program and Four Therapeutic Case Studies, *by Carmen G.L. Cummings, M.A.* This is an in-depth analysis of the techniques described in this book as they are applied in the Freedom from Fear of Flying seminars conducted in cities throughout the United States.*

Ms. Cummings has worked in these seminars with Truman W. Cummings over the past six years. She holds a Master's degree in counseling psychology from Vermont College of Norwich University in Montpelier, Vermont, and has served as a program advisor and instructor at Miami Dade Community College.

---

*Statistical analyses for this study computed by Alan Teich.

APPENDIX

The observations and conclusions that follow should provide hope and confidence to those who want to overcome their fear and should also prove interesting to professionals in related fields.

The Report

This study consists of two areas of research. The first area attempts to evaluate the efficacy of the procedures used in the Freedom from Fear of Flying program. The second part is a follow-up study that attempts to measure the long-term effect of the program on its participants.

Two groups of participants were studied. The "enrolled" group filled out questionnaires at the end of each seminar session. The "follow-up" group had participated in the seminar an average of seventeen months prior to completing the surveys. Of the 210 seminar participants, 61 percent were female and 39 percent male.

The majority of respondents in my survey (58 percent) were between the ages of thirty-six and fifty-five years, with an average age of forty-two years. In addition, 84 percent were married, 10 percent were single, and 3 percent were divorced (3 percent did not give their marital status). Many of the people (47 percent) had some educational experience at a college or university, and 26 percent had further education beyond the bachelor's degree.

The original intention of this study was to investigate four aspects of the Freedom from Fear of Flying (FFF) program:

A. Are FFF seminar graduates flying more often?
B. Are FFF seminar graduates and/or nongraduates (those who did not go on the graduation flight) flying with reduced anxietey symptoms?
C. Are FFF seminar graduates and/or nongraduates

using the techniques successfully in other fearful or phobic situations?

D. Assess the seminar effectiveness for the most valuable aspects.

A. *Frequency of flying.*

Data were not collected to discern specifically whether seminar graduates are flying more often than before participating in the seminar. However, information is available which would strongly suggest that this is the case. Participants from the "enrolled" group were asked if they were flying prior to taking the seminar. Thirty-eight percent said that they were flying, while 62 percent said they were not. When asked if they expected to fly following completion of the seminar, 84 percent said that they did expect to fly, while only 16 percent said that they did not have this expectation.

It is, of course, necessary to consider that these people would be likely to say that they expected to fly given that they decided to participate in the seminar. *However, from the 'follow-up" group, it was found that 88 percent reported that they were flying since completing the seminar.* Indeed, of those who said that they were still flying, 47 percent reported flying more than six times since the seminar. Although these results are statistically significant, they do not answer the question definitively since the comparison is made between two different groups. Thus, whereas a majority of the "enrolled" group said that they expected to fly, a similar percentage of the "follow-up" group of graduates reported that they were flying, indicating that expectations about flying would seem to be realistic.

Interestingly, the majority of these people (80 percent) did not seek further therapy for their fear of flying. Likewise, only 51 percent of the respondents said that they continued to use the seminar tapes to assist them in controlling their anxiety about flying. Of these people, significantly more reported using the tapes before flying (59 percent) than during flying (24 percent) or at other times. It is not surprising that the majority of those who still use the tapes, do so before flying. Based on the number of people who call us right before they fly, it is safe to say that one of the highest levels of fear occurs while they are *anticipating*. The remaining people (18 percent) said that they used the tapes at other times.

B. *Reduction of anxiety symptoms while flying.*

In order to assess whether seminar graduates were flying with reduced anxiety, reported anxiety levels for flying experiences after seminar graduation were obtained. An analysis of variance indicated significant differences among the reported levels of anxiety for the first, second, and third flying experiences after the seminar. There was greater reported anxiety during the first flight relative to the second and third flights, with these latter two not being statistically different in terms of reported anxiety.

C. *Use of seminar techniques in other fearful or phobic situations.*

Information was collected to discern whether seminar graduates used seminar techniques for other fear or phobic situations. Analysis revealed that a significantly larger number of people (78 percent) responded "yes" to this question. Of those who responded "yes," significantly more people (95 percent) reported that the techniques helped to decrease their anxiety feelings about other fearful situations relative to those who reported an increase in anxiety. This finding suggests that some of the people who attended the seminar are perceiving the techniques to be helpful and are practicing them on a regular basis. It is encouraging to know that such a large percentage of respondents are decreasing their levels of anxiety with the help of these techniques.

D. *Most valuable aspects of the seminar as anxiety reducers.*

Another area this study attempted to investigate was the

effectiveness of various components of the seminar: testimonials by graduates, practice with cassette tapes, circle discussion of feelings, education and films about flight procedures and flight safety, physical exercises to release tension, tour of airplanes, relaxation exercises, and the graduation flight. Results clearly show that *the graduation flight was viewed as high in reducing anxiety.* When compared with the other aspects of the seminar in terms of highly reducing anxiety, the graduation flight differed significantly from all other aspects except physical exercise, which was also rated highly. Most people (91 percent) viewed virtually all of the other aspects as being moderate in their ability to reduce anxiety for flying.

Thus, these data would suggest that the actual experience of flying provided the greatest reduction in flight anxiety, with physical exercise also being important in this process. This finding is particularly gratifying because the graduation flight is intended to have people cope most directly with their fear. In fact, most of the seminar serves to practice the skills necessary to cope with the anxious feelings when they arise. For the fearful flyer the anxious feelings peak just before flying and during the first few minutes of flight.

The respondents were asked whether they viewed their fear of flying as being based on rational and/or irrational beliefs. Interestingly, significantly more people believed their flying fear was based on both rational and irrational beliefs than rational beliefs alone. The number of people who reported that their fear was based on both beliefs did not significantly differ from those who believed the fear was based on irrational beliefs alone.

These fearful flyers were also asked to rate themselves on a number of personal and fear characteristics. Forty-eight percent viewed themselves as high on perfectionism and 52 percent believed that they were highly fearful of dying. Interestingly, significantly fewer people reported being moderately or highly fearful of elevators relative to slight fear.

However, significantly more people said that they were highly fearful of heights relative to moderate fear. In addition, most people (76 percent) reported that they were, in general, moderately or highly tense individuals. Again this is not surprising. It is fairly reasonable to assume that perfectionistic individuals as well as people with a strong fear of dying will be at least moderately tense.

Figure 1 indicates the degree of fear experienced by these people in response to particular aspects of flying. As can be seen in the figure (page 184), falling, crashing, and loss of control were rated as the most fearful events by a great percentage of the people.

It should be noted that these three fears are likely to be related to each other, and may be specific components of the general fear of losing control. The findings show that more than half of the people have a moderate fear of falling. This appears to confirm Dr. Ronell's opinion (in Diana M. Ronell, *Phobia: A Comparison of Uniphobic and Multiphobic Groups;* doctoral dissertation, Adelphi University; New York, 1977) that this fear is common among fearful flyers.

Being confined was also rated as highly fearful by a large percentage of respondents (46 percent). This is interesting when one considers that fear of elevators was rated as only slightly fear-producing by a preponderance of the respondents. This leads to speculation that the anxiety is not about being confined but about *where* the person is being confined.

Other noteworthy items that resulted in large percentages of high-fear responses include weather, takeoff, and the unknown.

Finally, information was gathered pertaining to flying fear in family members. Interestingly, there were significant differences in the number of people reporting flying fear in their fathers, mothers, and siblings. In particular, significantly more people reported that their fathers were fearful flyers (77 percent) than their mothers (19 percent) or their siblings (7 percent).

Summary, Conclusion, and Recommendations

The present study attempted to investigate the four aspects of the Freedom from Fear of Flying program, listed earlier in the Appendix, on pages 178–79.

The population in this study consisted of a "follow-up" group of 148 people who had taken the seminar an average of seventeen months previously and an "enrolled" group of 62 people who filled out evaluation surveys after each seminar session.

The findings are as follows:

A. From 148 seminar graduates it was found that 88 percent were flying since completing the seminar with 47 percent having flown more than six times since the graduation. In comparing the "follow-up" group and the "enrolled" group significantly more people reported flying after the seminar than before.

B. The finding on this item indicates that those who continued to fly were able to reduce their anxiety levels significantly in their second and third flights after the graduation flight. The first flight after the graduation flight showed higher levels of anxiety than their second and third flights. This is not surprising because this is the first flying experience since the seminar without the group support or leaders' guidance.

C. A large percentage of people (95 percent) responded that they use the seminar's techniques in other fearful situations and that these techniques are helpful in achieving a reduction of their anxiety levels. This is an encouraging finding. It is my opinion that, in general, most people tend to be inconsistent about practicing those very same techniques (exercise, diets, etc.) that are helpful.

D. As expected the most valuable aspects of the seminar, with significantly higher scores for anxiety reduction, were the graduation flight, followed by the physical exercises. The first finding (the graduation flight) supports Truman Cummings' opinion that fears, phobias, and their symptoms can only be overcome with the confrontation of the object or

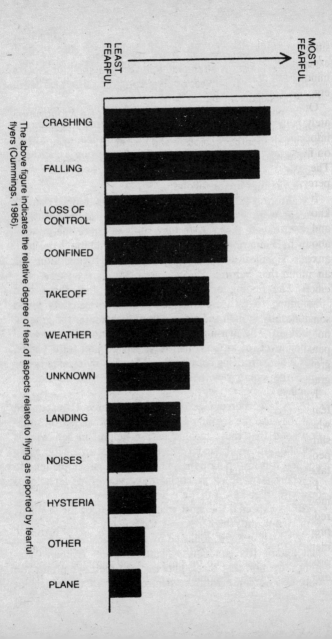

The above figure indicates the relative degree of fear of aspects related to flying as reported by fearful flyers (Cummings, 1986).

situation provoking it. The second finding was also to be expected. Movement reduces muscle tension and diverts the mind. Both these factors are necessary to help reduce anxiety.

Other aspects of the seminar that were reported as moderately helpful in coping with fear of flying were: educational information about flying, circle discussion on feelings, tapes on flying and fear, relaxation exercises, and group exercises. The graduation flight was viewed as most helpful by 94 percent of the respondents.

It is interesting to note that many people say they want to know more about flight safety, maintenance, pilot training, and other relevant information. Nonetheless, education about flying was reported as moderately helpful as an anxiety reducer. This is not surprising since education is an intellectual activity and the problem seems to be an emotional one.

Most questionnaire respondents included a variety of personal comments about the group and the leaders. Although no systematic analysis was done about these comments, personal accounts from many of the participants said that the group was a strong influence in their decision to take the graduation flight.

It is likely that fearful flyers are more ready to face their fear as a group. This dynamic is analogous to the dynamics of what social psychologists call the "risky shift." The "risky shift" refers to the phenomena that occur when as a group, people are likely to take more risks than each person would take as an individual.

Finally, even though the results of this investigation show moderate scores on most aspects of the seminar as anxiety reducers, it is my opinion that they are all a necessary preparation for the actual flight. Therefore, it is recommended that the FFF seminars continue using the same procedures in the same or similar order with the possible exception of the testimonials given by guest graduates. It is suggested that this aspect of the seminar be moved to the last session before the graduation flight.

The following three examples of seminar graduates are presented as evidence of the FFF techniques at work. They are taken directly from Ms. Cummings' experiences with specific fearful flyers, although their names have been changed to protect their anonymity. If you're a fearful flyer, perhaps these stories will offer you the hope of overcoming your fear and the motivation to go to work on it.

Sally had never flown comfortably. Her fear increased even though she had never had an accident or even an incident on an airplane. One day, Sally heard on the radio about the American Airlines crash in Chicago. She became quite alarmed thinking her husband might have taken that flight. Although he was not on that plane, Sally's husband had witnessed the crash. He was shocked and saddened by the experience, but it did not keep him from flying.

Sally, however, became more and more frightened and finally refused to fly at all and even avoided being near an airport. Her anxiety feelings escalated at the sight of an airplane or at the thought of flying.

In a flight that was to be Sally's last for five long years, she became so obviously distraught that the flight attendants became concerned about her. They tried to help her and calm her down as much as they could. They eventually asked the captain of the airplane if they could bring Sally to the cockpit. They did. Sally's anxiety subsided somewhat. She felt embarrassed and promised herself and others that she "would never fly" until she could manage or cope with her feelings more rationally.

Sally and her family moved to Florida from a northern city in 1981. She traveled by train and made several trips back and forth to New England by car or train.

Sally had registered in the FFF class in New York three years prior to her move to Florida. But she did not attend because it was "far for her to drive." While she was in New England attending a family wedding, her husband called her and notified her of an FFF seminar taking place in Miami and asked her if he should enroll her in it. She accepted.

Sally, a bright and dynamic woman, was skeptical and apprehensive during classes but also eager to cooperate and learn something that would help her fly again. She felt her life was handicapped by her inability to fly.

The last session of the FFF seminar was taking place inside a parked airplane. Sally's anxious feelings were obviously escalating as we approached the airport, and more so as we walked toward the parked airplane. She knew we were not going anywhere, yet her emotions were surfacing. She cried and shook as we walked down the connecting tunnel.

Sally is a rational and intelligent woman, but she could not control her feelings about this event. We walked down while all the time doing the exercises, breathing, and getting in touch with the physical aspects of the moment, rather than with her mental anticipations. She pounded the outside of the plane, felt it and smelled it, sat in a seat crying, and at the same time determined to follow procedures that she believed would diminish her anxiety. Finally she calmed down. She got up and walked around, starting to familiarize herself with the object of her fear, the plane. The next day, Sally flew in the graduation flight. It was not easy for her, but her courage and persistence helped her.

Since then Sally flies an average of six times a year, making more than fifty flights since she graduated in the FFF seminar. She is comfortable flying 90 percent of the time, and the rest of the time, she says, her discomforts are due to more common reactions: irritation at delays, boredom on long flights, occasional fatigue, and so on. Sally says she used the suggested relaxation techniques in other areas of her life successfully.

APPENDIX

* * *

Ann came to the FFF seminars with mixed emotions. In previous years she had worked very hard to conquer her agoraphobia. The fear of flying was a residual fear, and she was quite skeptical about whether she could overcome it.

During the seminar sessions, Ann's questions seemed to be largely motivated by her fear. She persistently spoke as if she would not be able to make the flight. She doubted the efficacy of the group sessions and her own ability to conquer this nagging fear in spite of all her previous successes.

By the third meeting Ann seemed encouraged and more optimistic, though she still projected ahead to the day of the flight with fear and doubt. It was apparent that she wanted to fly with the group on the graduation flight but that involuntary thoughts were creating some of the old dreaded feelings.

The day of the flight Ann arrived nervous and anxious. She displayed an enormous amount of determination and bravery when she, in spite of her feelings, continued to practice the new coping techniques she had acquired. When we boarded the airplane, Ann looked quite distraught. While we were waiting for the other passengers to board, she started shaking, perspiring, and crying. She kept repeating over and over again that she "had to get off." She thought she was reaching the point of panic, and although I suspected that if she stayed, she would soon be over it, I reminded her that the decision was hers and that she was free to get off because the door of the plane was still open.

But Ann had another part of her that advised her differently. Dr. Claire Weekes, a pioneer in the study and treatment of agoraphobia and author of several major works in the field, calls it "the inner voice." She did not move from her seat. By now the door of the plane was closed. We started taxiing. Ann wept profusely, shook, and perspired. I held her hand. We took off, and for the first few minutes, I could feel her anxiety escalating. And then, as if by a miracle, she started breathing more slowly and deeply. Her perspiration and shaking stopped. Her expression changed from terror to awe. We were a few minutes in the air when Ann, still crying, though now softly, said that she had just remembered how much she used to love to fly.

Since the graduation flight, Ann has flown several times. During her last flight, her young daughter wrote us a postcard thanking us for what we did for her mommy.

Occasionally Ann says she is apprehensive before a flight and sometimes even during it. But she says she practices her techniques and listens to the tapes. Her fear of flying no longer controls her. Ann has enhanced her life and that of her family by conquering her fear of flying.

A young businessman named Loren had not been on a plane sober for several years. When he stopped drinking, he stopped flying. In 1982, after five years of sobriety, he fell off the wagon at the terrifying thought of a long flight overseas, where he was being sent by his employers. He consumed so much alcohol before and during the flight that when he arrived at his destination, he had to be hospitalized. After several days in the hospital, he went back to the U.S. sedated and accompanied by an attendant. He was not able to perform his business assignment and afterwards went through some horrifying months of excessive alcohol intoxication. When he broke through that period and sobered up, he decided he would never fly again rather than risk going back to drinking.

When Loren enrolled in the FFF seminar, he had been sober for some time. Two days before the graduation flight, he asked me for a private appointment. It was during the appointment that I learned about his experience with alcohol as a consequence of his fear about that flight in 1982. He also said he had a fear of bridges and tunnels, which he had been avoiding for several years. Before the session was over he understood that the only way to get rid of his fear of bridges and tunnels was by starting to use them. He decided to confront this fear and asked me to accompany him as he drove over the bridge between Detroit and Windsor, Canada. Loren seemed determined to go through the experience of crossing a bridge no matter what it entailed.

We started on our way to Windsor. He was driving, and we kept noting billboards and identifying the surroundings and his feelings to avoid anticipatory anxiety. We reached the entrance to the bridge and stopped for a few minutes while he identified his feelings and took a few deep breaths. We started to cross. He seemed to be doing well until we had to stop behind a line of cars to pay the toll. We were in the outside lane and could see a large body of water when his feelings of fear intensified. His breathing became shallow and fast, and he felt pressure on his chest; he thought he was having a heart attack. That thought itself elevated his feelings of anxiety. I followed the regular procedures used in most phobic situations including the imaginary scale from one to ten to measure his anxiety. We did this many times, he calmed down, and we crossed to the other side. Then he stopped the car and cried and laughed for a while. I think it was this man's determination to endure any amount of fear or pain that made his success possible.

After that ordeal, he was so exhilarated that he kept repeating, "I feel like a million bucks." After crossing the bridge, he felt he "could conquer anything" and decided to return to Detroit through the tunnel. I suggested we stop and practice some of the procedures, but he assured me it was not necessary. He did a few deep breathing exercises, measured his anxiety level (all on his own), and said, "It's a two." We crossed, and he was quite at ease.

He was very nervous again on the day of the graduation flight. He said he wanted to do it himself, but that if he felt he was going to need a drink, he would ask me for help. We took off. He followed the procedures on his own. Occasionally he would reach for my or someone else's hand in the group. He shook often and cried some, but he made it.

Since then, Loren has been promoted in his job, and during 1985 and part of 1986, he flew to London, Brussels, Amsterdam, and Nice. He has flown to a dozen different cities in the U.S. and Canada, has traveled in a helicopter, and has made a trip on a small Cessna plane, something, he says, "I had sworn I would never do."

Recently, Loren was on a flight that was held circling over New York airspace for an hour and a half due to traffic congestion. He was so relaxed that he fell asleep.

This man's story is inspiring. To me it depicts the resiliency, the courage, and the possibilities that are in so many of us just waiting to be tapped.

Loren, with the help of AA, the FFF seminars, some supportive individuals, and his own faith, has conquered his fears and is now truly "flying high."